Pictured Key
Nature Series

D0904554

How To Know

THE
ECONOMIC
PLANTS

An illustrated key for identifying the plants used by man for food and in other personal ways, with some essential facts about each plant.

H. E. JAQUES

Professor Emeritus of Biology
Iowa Wesleyan College

wcb

WM. C. BROWN COMPANY PUBLISHERS
Dubuque, Iowa

Some one has suggested that we show the pronounci-
ation of our name. It doesn't make much difference, for
even our friends have several forms for it. — but here
it is:

Jaques — Jā'-kwis

THE PICTURED-KEY NATURE SERIES

How To Know The—

CONTENTS

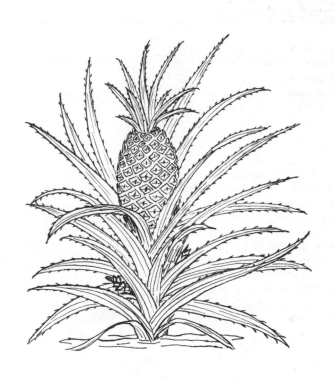

INTRODUCTION

 title could have several different applications. It has been chosen to confine the treatment of "economic plants" to the species having a close personal relationship to man. Accordingly the plants which supply us with food and fibers have been selected for identification by by the well-known Picture-Key treatment. Surely, every one wishes to recognize and understand the plants which thus touch his life so vitally.

"Where and when do we eat?" is an urgent question not only with man but also with all of the more than one million species of known animals. The green plants have the contract for supplying the sustenance of all living things, both plant and animal. These some 275,000 species of green plants must not only build their own tissues from the inorganic elements with which they are surrounded but they must, directly or indirectly, furnish every bit of the organic materials which around 120,000 species of non-green plants and the over 1,000,000 known species of animals require in order to live and grow.

Practically every species of green plant helps feed other plants and animals, but it is surprising that man restricts himself to the use of but a small percentage of all these available plants. Well over 500 families of plants are listed in "Plant Families—How to Know Them," yet the plants seriously used for food by civilized man fall in only 72 of those families. It seems likely that fully 95% of man's plant foods come from representatives of only five plant families.

Only a very small percentage of plants are poisonous. Almost all of the others would supply considerable nutriment even though not tasty. Primitive peoples and pioneers have sustained themselves on many of these out of necessity. We have made no effort to include such plants.

This is a revision of "Plants We Eat and Wear" which was published in 1943. The nomenclature has been brought up to date, some additional plants pictured and described and many other changes made.

* * * * *

Numerous friends have helped in the preparation of the book as it now stands. The drawings have been made by Francesca Jaques Stoner, Mary Hinkle, Martha Jaques Cutkomp and Joan Sturtevant. We are grateful to all who have helped in any way; and especially to the many nature lovers and teachers who write to say encouraging things about the Pictured-Key Nature books.

March, 1958

SOME HELPFUL FACTS ABOUT PLANTS

KNOWLEDGE of plant structures and of plant classification is necessary to make any intelligent study of plants. Without teaching a whole course in botany, we will attempt to explain some things the reader should find helpful as he continues his study of economic plants.

The world's grand array of some 393,000 different plants which are now known to science divides rather naturally into four great divisions. Let's show this graphically. Fig. 1. More than half of these plants bear flowers and seeds; the others do not. These others usually have single celled "spores" for their reproduction. We'll mark off a section then, and label it "Spermatophyta (The Seed-bearing Plants) 250,700+." Fig. 1.

If a city is to attain size it must have adequate water, sewerage and transportation systems that extend to all parts of it. That is equally true for plants. In them these three systems are combined and known as *fibrovascular-bundles*. The seed-bearing plants, of course, are thus equipped, but another group, the ferns, also have vascular bundles. That gives us our second division which we will label "Pteridophyta (Ferns, etc.) 10,000+." All these interesting plants have vascular bundles but do not have seeds.

Now, the going gets more technical. The seed plants and the ferns, and also some others, reproduce by an egg which is in a cellular flask-shaped structure that botanist call an *archegonium*. Many very simple plants on the other hand produce eggs that are surrounded only by a non-cellular cell wall and have never known an archegonium. This gives us a natural separation for the remaining plants. Those with archegonia (but no vascular bundles) we will label "Bryophyta (Mosses and Liverworts) 23,000." All the remaining plants, — the "have-nots" — which have no archegonia, no vascular bundles and no seeds, we'll call "Thallophyta (Algae and

Figure 1

Fig. 1. The whole Plant Kingdom (392,700+ different plants) divided proportionately into its four great divisions. a, representing 287 seed-bearing plants used for food, described in this book; b, seed-bearing plants used for fibers, etc. (19); c, Sturtevant's maximum number of food plants, all divisions (4233); d, algae and fungi used for food, (15).

1

Fungi) 110,000+." This last group is an exceedingly important one but man uses only a very few of the plants within it for his food.

We make but very scant use of the Ferns or of the Mosses for food. But the Seed-bearing Plants—that is different—how very much we depend upon them!

HOW WE FEEL ABOUT FOOD

The trend of thought about our food has undergone some radical changes in recent years. Not long ago the chief emphasis with foods was taste and perhaps next its appearance. Now we hear much about better health, physical appearance, and vitality. Foods are selected and recommended for the nutriment man's digestive system can take from them. The discussion runs to calories, minerals and vitamins with the result that many of us are eating the foods we once disliked, because they provide the desired vitamins and minerals or enable us to maintain the proper weight.

Bailey in his inventories lists 247 vegetables and 161 fruits, a total of 408, eaten some where the world around.

Sturtevant, who some years ago made a list of the cultivated food plants of the world, named 1070 species but went on to say that he had noted a total of 4233 plants which were used some where and some how for food.

These larger lists which are still surprisingly small as compared with the total species of known plants, include many plants practically unknown in our country and numbers of others ("weeds" to the layman) which are non-poisonous and nutritive of course, but only occasionally included in a mess of greens or tried for jellies, preserves, etc. for the novelty of the thing.

The whole food problem boils down to this,—*The green plants first make their own food and grow, so that they can then feed the entire living world.* Let us see just how they"make their own food" and what they do with it.

HOW PLANTS FEED AND GROW

A growing green plant is truthfully said to be the "greatest factory in the world." It is a factory where chemical activities are busily transforming available compounds or elements into new compounds in some marvelous ways and with a mass production that puts our assembly lines to shame.

The raw materials needed are few and almost everywhere abundant. Practically all of the many products the plant makes are made from ten elements. Carbon, Oxygen, Hydrogen, Nitrogen, Phosphorus, Sulphur, Iron, Magnesium, Calcium and Potassium. Other elements may play their part in very small portions in some plant products, but the 10 just named are the elements that figure most largely in plant growth.

The plant begins its work with the first three elements named above. Hydrogen and oxygen are taken in through the roots in the form of water, (H_2O). Carbon and oxygen are taken into the leaves from the surrounding air as a gas, carbon dioxide (CO_2). The power is sun-light. It is wireless. It streams into the factory with high efficiency and is not even metered. Innumerable tiny green bodies within the cells of the leaf make up the personnel. With a bit of plant magic which botanist call *photosynthesis*, these very simple, thin and highly abundant substances,—water and carbon dioxide, are fused into a new product, *glucose*, one of the sugars. Chemically it is expressed thus: $6 CO_2 + 6 H_2O \rightarrow C_6H_{12}O_6 + 6 O_2$ (six molecules of carbon dioxide + six molecules of water yield by this change one molecule of glucose plus six molecules of oxygen). This extra oxygen is interesting and very important. It is put back into the air and is used again by animals and plants in *respiration*. Thus the green plants of country and town, —park or window box—are releasing oxygen into the surrounding air throughout the lighted hours and so making the air more healthful. That is why we put some green aquatic plants in our fish bowl. The plant gives off

Figure 2. Photosynthesis of plants, and respiration of plants and animals balance the air and water for healthful living.

3

oxygen in its photosynthesis which is dissolved into the water. The fish utilizing this oxygen for its respiration, returns carbon dioxide to the water which, of course, may be used by the plants again for photosynthesis. Both the fish and the plants prosper and we term it a balanced aquarium.

The energy of the sun is required to compound the glucose. This energy is released again when the glucose or some later plant product made from it, is broken down by respiration. And thus the fish gets its power to move and grow, and we maintain our body temperature of 98.6 F., and get the necessary energy to work and play and to think through pages like these.

The plant, still utilizing the sun's energy, directly or indirectly, can shift the proportions of the elements in the glucose and change it into many similar compounds such as cane sugar ($C_6 H_{22} O_{11}$) or starch ($C_6 H_{10} O_5$) or by more radical shifts, into fats and oils, all of which also contain only these three elements. A typical fat formula is that of palmitin ($C_{51} H_{98} O_6$). Since it takes additional sun-energy to change carbo-hydrates into fats, it is apparent that fats when broken down by respiration will release more energy than can be had from carbohydrates.

MAKING PLANT PROTEINS

Proteins contain not only carbon, hydrogen, and oxygen, as do fats but also nitrogen and usually either phosphorus or sulphur or both. The plant of course makes its own proteins by building over carbohydrates and adding the necessary new elements. Protein compounds are very complex. Typical formulas to illustrate this are *gliadin*, a wheat protein, ($C_{685} H_{1068} N_{196} O_{211} S_5$) and *casein* from milk, ($C_{708} H_{1130} N_{180} O_{224} S_4 P_4$). The living protoplasm of plant and animal cells is formed of proteins. Since it seems that plant proteins are the original source of all animal proteins these plant compounds assume increased significance.

The other elements already referred to become parts of some special plant products.

MOVEMENTS OF PLANT FOODS

Just as a commercial factory has its pipe lines, belt lines or other schemes of transportation to bring in raw materials and to move the finished product to storage, plants are likewise equipped. Since all plant products, raw or finished, are moved as liquids, pipe lines suffice. Water containing the needed plant foods dissolved in it, is taken into the tiny root tips by osmotic pressure and shortly finds its way into small tubes made from elongated cylindrical plant cells placed end to end. As the tiny roots unite into larger roots, the tubes collect into larger bundles so that when the several large roots fuse into the plant stem

many fibro-vascular bundles, each with several to numerous liquid-carrying tubes are running parallel through the length of the stem. These again separate as they pass into the branches of the plant. A few pass out each leaf, flower or fruit stem, and then split up more and more until all parts of the leaf, flower or fruit are served. The veins seen in leaves contain these bundles. Some of the tubes carry raw materials into the leaves and other tubes in the same bundle will transport organized foods out of the leaf.

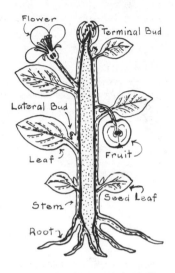

Figure 3. Diagram of plant to show parts and the vascular system. Solid lines to carry liquids up; dotted lines carrying them down.

Most of the photosynthesis of foods goes on in the leaves, although any green plant-part such as green stems, green fruit, or even green tubers will be doing their quota of this important work. During the day the leaves fill up with the foods being organized within them. Day and night the pipe lines are carrying this away to the ware-houses for storage or to parts of the plant where these organized foods are being built into new plant parts. Simple sugar or starch tests can be made which reveal that leaves contain much more starch and sugar towards the end of a day than at its beginning.

FOOD STORAGE

Plants usually store food to provide for a time when the plant will need it. Fleshy *tap roots* such as beets, fleshy *lateral roots* as the sweet potato, thick stems as in Kohlrabi, *tubers* (special stems) as the Irish

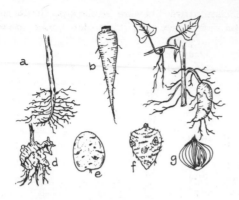

Figure 4. Special storage organs. a, fibrous roots; b, fleshy taproot c, fleshy lateral root; d, rhizome (fleshy stem); e, tuber (fleshy stem); f, corm (fleshy stem); g, bulb (fleshy leaves).

potato, *rhizomes* (root like stems) as in ginger, thick *leaf-stems* as rhubarb and *seeds* are examples. These serve the plant for reproduction, or for quick growth in emergencies. All seeds contain sufficient food materials to supply the young plant till it can get on its own. Man has learned to take these for his own use. He is a robber when he does so because the plants meant them for themselves. If he is smart, he will not take all of them, or at least will make some adequate provision for assuring a big crop again and again. Only "dummies" kill the goose that lays the golden eggs, or digs wild orchids or other rare plants.

MANY HELPERS AND THEIR PAY

Plants have helpers for some jobs and are often willing to pay well for the work. Birds and other animals are engaged to scatter plant

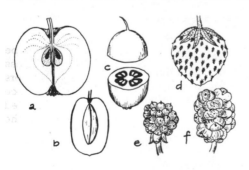

Figure 5. Some types of Fleshy Fruits. a, pome; b, drupe; c, berry; d, fleshy receptacle; e, aggregate fruit; f, multiple fruit.

seeds. Such seeds are often enclosed in tasteful nutritious fruit in which much food material is stored. Blackberries and wild grapes, for instance, are widely scattered by birds dropping the undigested seeds Larger fruits are carried away to be eaten in a secluded spot and the seeds rejected. Man makes good food uses of these fruits and has greatly improved them by selection and breeding.

Fleshy leaves and stems are designed as storage organs but even slender parts may contain much food acceptable to man, as well as

6

the vitamins we watch for. Just as we wish to give the best we possess to our children, so plants turn their most concentrated foods into their flowers and seeds. A seed is a young plant (embryo) which has enough concentrated food stored with it to provide nutriment for the little plant until it can establish a root system, become green and make an adequate amount of food to supply its own needs. Part of this rich supply of food is in the cotyledons or seed leaves.

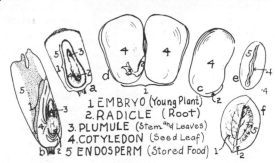

1 EMBRYO (Young Plant)
2. RADICLE (Root)
3. PLUMULE (Stem and Leaves)
4.COTYLEDON (Seed Leaf)
5 ENDOSPERM (Stored Food)

Figure 6. Typical seeds, and their parts. a, kernel of corn; b, transverse section of kernel of corn; c, Lima bean with seed coat removed; d, bean with cotyledons spread apart. Castor bean with seed coat removed; e edge view; f, face view with half of endosperm removed

These cotyledons are a part of the embryo. Often an endosperm surrounds the embryo. It is simply a mass of stored food which the young plant after it has started to grow digests and uses to build its own tissues. In seeds like the bean, the endosperm has been consumed and made a part of the cotyledons before the seed ripens. There is no endosperm but instead two large cotyledons in beans. These supply food to the young plant. Corn, a monocotyledon has, of course, only one cotyledon. A very large percentage of the plant foods utilized by man, around the world, comes from seeds.

PLANT POISONS

While the eating of plants is being discussed something should be said of plant poisons. Just as man puts barbed wire or electric fences around his belongings, plants have found it necessary to erect barriers with the result that some plants are thorn covered and in consequence are untouched by grazing animals. Other plants have been protected by poisons. On the whole, however, this is a friendly world and the percentage of poisonous plants is small.

PLANT FIBERS

Out of necessity primitive man was likely a big eater long before he gave much thought to things to wear, and even when he put on clothes for protection or ornament it was easier to kill than to weave. His first clothing was likely skins of other animals, but presently he learned to make fabrics from plant fibers, and to ornament them with plant dyes.

7

Plant fibers are twisted into thread and woven into fabrics. Some of these fibers surround seeds to enable them to be wind disseminated. Man removes these threads and uses them for twisting without needing to give them much special treatment. Cotton is an outstanding example.

The stems of many species of plants contain long, very slim heavy walled fibers to give strength to the stem. These bast fibers are removed from the stem by "retting," (putting in water or laid out to take the dew) or by a mechanical process, smoothed up, bleached, twisted into threads and woven. Linen from flax and ramie from an Indian plant illustrate this type. Fibers are also taken from the leaves of some plants.

Thick milky juice (*latex*) as found in some plants is collected and processed to form a tough water-proof material. Rubber from several plant sources illustrates this method. It and similar preparations are usually spread on a base of cotton or other fiber materials to give strength to the product.

Rayon threads are made from plant parts that are extensively processed. Many other synthetic fibers now extensively used in making fabrics are derived, directly or indirectly from plant sources.

FLOWER PATTERNS

For the reader whose botanical training is limited, perhaps we should say a bit about flowers since flower structures are used so largely in determining plants. *Complete* flowers have four parts (all of which are modified leaves) arising in whorls from the end of a stem, the *pedicel*.

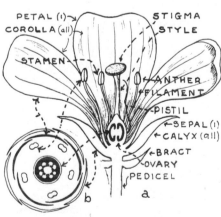

The expanded end of this stem is known as the *receptacle*. Going up the pedicel, the first whorl of parts is the *calyx* made up of *sepals*. (Occasionally flowers have a series of leaf-like bracts below their calyx which could be mistaken for sepals.) The sepals enclose the bud and protect its more delicate parts and are usually green in color, though not necessarily so. The next whorl is the *corolla*, and its parts the *petals*. Petals are often brilliantly colored and f a n c i f u l l y

Figure 7. a, longitudinal section of a flower naming its parts; b, floral diagram of the same flower.

marked. They attract insects and other pollinators. The petals of a corolla may be united with each other to form a tube; the same is true of sepals. *Stamens* come next. They are the male reproductive parts and produce *pollen* in their *anthers*. *Filaments* are usually present to hold the anthers out from the walls of the flower. At the center of the flower perched on the end of the *pedicel* is the *pistil*. It is made up of *ovary*, *style* and *stigma*. It is the female part of the flower. In each of one or more cavities of the ovary are borne one or more ovules. The stigma at the topmost part of the pistil is a special organ for receiving the pollen grains. It is usually separated from the ovary by a longer or short stem known as the style. Through the action of wind, insects or some other agency, pollen is transferred from anthers to stigmas. This process is *pollination*. The pollen grain then grows a tube which penetrating the stigma style and ovary, searches out an ovule and breaking into it releases a sperm nucleus which fuses with the egg nucleus of the ovule. This process is known as *fertilization*. When it transpires successfully the ovule develops into

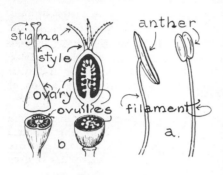

Figure 8. a, stamens showing parts; b, pistils dissected to show parts.

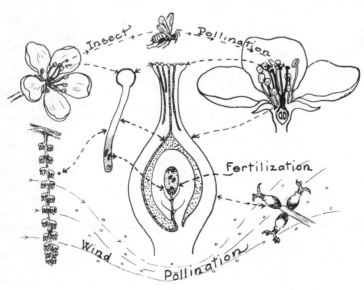

Figure 9. Pollination and fertilization work like this.

9

a *seed* and the ovary containing the ovule becomes a *fruit*. Only one or two or three of these parts are present in some ("*incomplete*") flowers. Flowers with both stamens and pistils are said to be *perfect* while if but one or the other of these "*essential organs*" are represented in the flower it is *imperfect*. The whole story would cover several additional pages but this should enable the novice to get started. The study of plants is interesting and we recommend it just for the fun it offers. Some other terms relating to plant structures are defined in the glossary.

ABOUT PLANT NAMES

Every one of the nearly 400,000 plants known to live on the earth has a scientific name, which should be the same in all languages and in all parts of the world. Many of the better known plants also have common names,—often several of them for one plant, which may make the understanding difficult.

Throughout the book and in the "List" (p. 155) it will be noted that emphasis has been given to the common name of each plant but that its scientific name has been added, for in many cases that is the only way one can be sure just which plant is being discussed.

Scientific names always begin with a capitalized word. It is the genus name. Closely similar plants fall in the same genus and related genera belong to a "family." The second word is the species name. We begin it with a small letter. A third,—a variety name is sometimes included. A scientific name is followed by the name (or its abbreviation) of the scientist who gave this name to the plant. It is called the "authority" or "author."

Take "Dent Corn" for an example; it is but one of six varieties of *Zea* (genus) *mays* (species) L. (authority). Its full scientific name is *Zea mays indentata* Bailey. That tells us Bailey devised this three-word name (trinomial) and that the variety name is "indentata." Scientific names are printed in italic type or underscored, but the authority name is not italicized. Linnaeus who originated the binomial system, gave names to all the plants he knew. Leaf through a botany manual and note the plants bearing L. as an authority name. Linnaeus was the first to name corn. He called it *Zea mays* so that is followed by L. as an authority name. The variety names of Indian corn have been named by later authors as the authority names indicate.

HOW TO USE THE KEYS

ONE is often tempted to locate plants in a book like this, by leafing through and looking at the pictures. That may not be bad for much can be learned in that way. The experienced botanist or zoologist sometimes saves much time in his identification work by turning to a group to which knows his plant must belong, then by comparing pictures, selects a few species which represent all the ones which his unknown specimen could possibly be. From there it is a simple matter to carefully compare the key characters with his specimen and the determination is made.

Well planned identification keys make the naming of plants or animals comparatively simple and accurate. Young nature lovers should train themselves to handle keys with ease and precision.

We see in a greenhouse a strange, coarse vine bearing several large somewhat banana-shaped fruits, 10 to 12 inches long, which are said to be edible. How can our key help us?

Starting at the first of the key at page 12 we compare 1a with 1b and noting the flowers on our plant, assign it to 1a and see at the right of the page that we are referred to the 8th pair of statements. Comparing 8a with 8b we find that our plant is an "Angiosperm" which takes us to 10. Examining the plant again, we see that while the leaves are long and broad and punctured with slits and holes, all the veins run somewhat parallel to each other. Its others characters also mark it as a "Monocotyledon." 11b next directs us to 29. Since the leaves are not palm-like we find 32a directing us to 33 where it fits 33b and seems to be a Ceriman. We next check with the description and figure and see that we are doubtless right.

As you work with these keys you will find that many plants appear at two or more places in the key. Many species have been keyed both by their use and by their botanical characters to make their determination easier. If you are not a botanist look up the unfamiliar terms in the illustrated glossary at the back and the rest should be comparatively easy.

PICTURED-KEYS FOR IDENTIFYING
THE ECONOMIC PLANTS

2b Microscopic single celled plants used to raise bread; eaten for their vitamins. Fig. 10.........YEAST *Saccharomyces cerevisiae* (Han.)

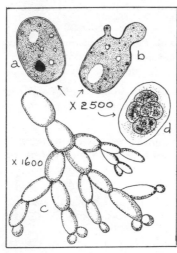

a, single plant; b, cell producing two buds; c, a colony of budded cells; d, a cell containing four resting spores (ascospores within an ascus).

There are many species of yeasts but this one which is used rather exclusively in bread-making and beer-brewing is the most important. Yeast plants grow and multiply by budding. Resting spores are also formed sometimes within a cell. This type of spore formation shows the yeasts to be Ascomycetes.

Yeasts are rich in vitamins and are often prescribed to correct a vitamin deficiency.

Figure 10

Yeasts change sugars into carbon dioxide and alcohol. It is this gas that makes dough rise and gives the effervescence to fermented beverages. Wild yeasts of numerous species are abundant and widely distributed. The wild yeasts found on the skins of fruit bring about prompt fermentation when the juice is extracted from such fruit. "Salt-rising" bread depends upon wild yeasts and bacteria for its leavening.

It is interesting to note that the superiority of wheat flour for bread-making is due to the greater percentage of gluten it contains. The gluten holds the carbon dioxide gas until the bread raises and is baked. Kneeding the bread dough breaks the large gas bubbles up into many tiny ones which makes the bread finer grained. Flours that are short of gluten, such as corn meal, cannot hold the gas and do not raise well.

3a Much branched marine plants, yellowish-brown, or reddish-purple. 4

3b Land plants, some without chlorophyll.........................5

12

4a Mostly a Pacific Ocean red alga, without an auxillary cell (separate vegetative cell which receives the zygote nucleus in its migration from the carpoganium). Primary branching not dichotomous. Fig. 11.
..........................AGAR-AGAR *Gelidium cartilagineum* Gaill.

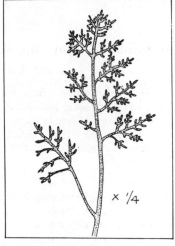

× ¼

Figure 11

This is one of several species of red algae from which Agar-Agar is extracted. These plants grow abundantly in the Pacific along both the Asiatic and American coasts. Agar is used in soups, jellies, ice cream and medicines, usually to give bulk. It is employed in the textile industry and has proved an ideal solidifier for culture media used in the study of bacteria since its melting point is higher than that of gelatine.

It has been produced largely by the Japanese. In more recent years it has been gathered and extracted in our country, but the higher labor costs have resulted in much of it now being imported from Japan and Mexico. Some members of the genus are found in the Atlantic. This product is also known as vegetable-isinglass, Ceylon moss or Chinese moss.

4b Red algae growing mostly along the shores of the North Sea and the Atlantic coast. Primary branching dichotomous. Usually shorter than 4a. An auxillary cell present. Fig. 12......................
IRISH MOSS (a) *Chondrus crispus* Stac. (b) *Gigartina stellata* Batters

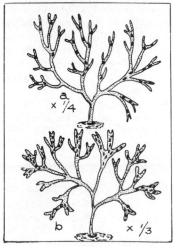

a × ¼

b × ⅓

Figure 12

Both of these red algae have flattened, some-what ribbon-like thalli. They are attached to the rocks by branched root-like structures. After being collected the plants are put through several turns of washing and drying. This Irish Moss or Carragheen, as it is sometimes called, is made into a jelly or by using more water into a beverage.

The quantity of marine algae is unlimited, but since its nutritive value for man is comparatively low, only a few species are much used for food. These plants have been collected for many years off the New England coast.

5a (b,c) Fairly large, green plants with finely divided, fern-like leaves; stems mostly under ground. TRUE FERNS.....................7

5b Whitish, fleshy fruiting bodies growing on the ground or on decaying plants; never contain green chlorophyll; reproducing by spores 6

5c Small grayish-green leaf-like plants growing on the ground. Spores born in shallow cups. Fig. 13....................................
........................ICELAND MOSS *Cetraria islandica* Ach.

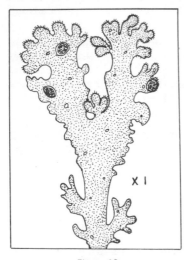

X 1

Figure 13

This lichen, rather common in Iceland and Norway is dried, ground into flour and used for bread making. It is also made into jelly or a beverage.

The *Manna-Lichen* grows in large patches on stones in the deserts of Africa and Asia and is similarly used for food. Danish brandy is made from the *Reindeer-Lichen*. That species grows at its best in the far North but is often found on barren hill-tops in temperate regions, ROCK TRIPE (2 or 3 species), large, leaf-like lichens, are sometimes eaten. They are found in our eastern mountains and in the North.

Lichens would likely rate as the world's sturdiest plants. They are really a dual partnership in which an algal plant has joined forces with a fungus, each helping the other. For sheer hardiness and resistance to unfavorable conditions they have no equal.

6a A mushroom with sponge-like cap; spores born in cavities on outside of cap. Fig. 14...COMMON MOREL *Morchella esculenta* **Pers.**

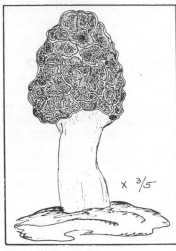

x $^3/_5$

Figure 14

Some folks call this and the several related species "Sponge Mushrooms" and make them the only ones they will collect to eat. The other mushrooms are Basidiomycetes (bearing their spores on clubs) but the Morels are Ascomycetes. Their spores are borne in microscopic sacks, each usually containing eight spores. They are found sometimes in great abundance in low wooded areas. The honey-combed caps are yellowish-brown while the stems are nearly white. The flesh is fairly heavy and requires longer cooking than many mushrooms.

No Morels are known to be poisonous. Because of their many cavities they need to be carefully inspected as they may harbor insects.

6b Mushrooms with umbrella like head, pink gills, a collar around the stem and without a volva. Fig. 15.........................
.................COMMON MUSHROOM *Agaricus campestris* **L.**

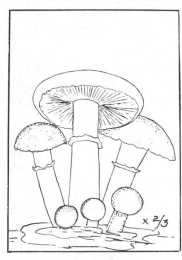

x $^2/_3$

Figure 15

This is the usual species of mushroom sold on the market. It is frequently found in late summer and fall growing in fields. The gills are at first pink but turn brown when they age.

The vegatative part of these plants consists of many white threads (*mycelia*) growing through the ground where their nutriment is absorbed from decaying organic matter. Cultivated mushrooms are raised in caves or buildings where the temperature and humidity can be controlled. Pieces of spawn (mycelia) are planted in manure-enriched beds. When they first come up the head entirely surrounds the stem. They are then known as buttons.

There are hundreds of species of wild mushrooms which are edible and only a comparatively few which are poisonous. Since the poisonous ones are so deadly no one should ever gather and eat mushrooms unless he is sure of the species he has collected. There are much quicker methods of dying but few that are more certain or painful.

Many persons use the term "toadstool" in speaking of poisonous species. Botanists have no such distinction.

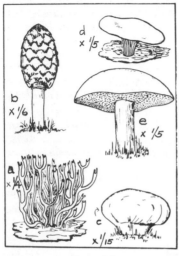

Figure 16

A few of the common edible wild species are being pictured. Unless you know your mushrooms DO NOT collect something that may somewhat resemble these drawings and feed them to your family. Even only one or two poisonous ones among many edible specimens may have fatal results.

Fig. 16. Some edible mushrooms. a, *Coral Fungus*, white, yellow or pink; b, *Shaggy Mane*, several inches high, much prized; c, *Puffball*, all puffballs are safe, but break them open to be sure they are puffballs; d, *Oyster Mushroom*, white or cream, grows on trees; c, *Edible Boletus*, red-brown on top, greenish beneath.

7a Large coarse fern with all the leaves similar, usually twice pinnate; spore cases (sori) (c) borne in a continuous line at the margin of the leaflets. Fig. 17....BRACKEN-FERN *Pteridium aquilinum* Kuhn.

Figure 17

a, small section of leaf; b, leaflet with sori (c) at margin; d, young leafstock (crosier).

We ordinarily do not think of ferns being used for food. There are a few exceptions.

The bracken (also known as Eagle-Fern, Pasture-Brake etc.) is widely distributed throughout our country. It spreads by long, branching rootstocks which creep under ground. The leaves are triangular in outline, sometimes 4 ft. long and 3 ft. in width.

The young leaf stalks, with unrolled croziers (Fig. 17d), are eaten; cooked like asparagus or green beans. Older parts should not be eaten.

16

7b A coarse fern bearing 2 distinct types of leaves; spore-bearing (fertile) leaves (a) and sterile (vegetative) leaves (b). Fig. 18......
.........................OSTRICH-FERN *Pteretis pensylvanica* Fern.

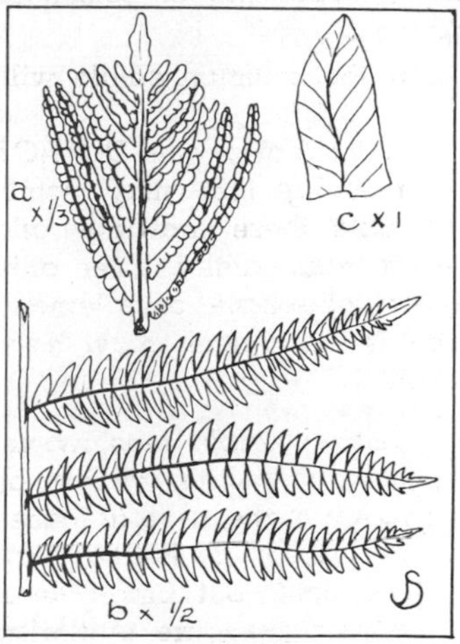

Figure 18

The sterile leaves of this vigorously growing fern may attain a length of 7 ft. The fertile leaves are seldom much over a foot in height. They are dark brown. Their sole function is to bear spores.

The tender parts of the young sterile leaves are eaten like green beans or asparagus, but older leaves should not be used.

The SENSITIVE FERN, a much smaller plant (2 ft. or less) is somewhat similar in general appearance. The leaf veins anastomose in contrast to the Ostrich-Fern in which the veins are free (c). It is somewhat poisonous and should not be eaten.

8a Seeds enclosed within an ovary (becoming a dry or fleshy fruit). Fig. 19a.....
The ANGIOSPERMS....10

8b Seeds borne u n d e r the dry cones. Fig. 19b....9
.....The GYMNOSPERMS

Figure 19

THE GYMNOSPERMS

9a Palm-like or fern-like plants with pinnate leaves. CYCADS. Fig. 20.
...........................SAGO-PALM *Cycas revoluta* Thunb.

This is not a palm but a cycad. It is a common ornamental in the South and is seen growing in tubs where the winters are too severe for outdoor growing. The plant may attain a height of 10 feet with leaves 2-7 ft. long. Several species of cycads are grown but this is the most common. Sago, a granular starch, used in puddings, etc. is made from the pith of this and other cycads as well as some palms. The seeds are eaten by the natives.

The seeds are borne in large cones (b), with two seeds (d), borne under

Figure 20

each scale (c). The male plants produce the staminate cones which bear pollen sacks on the under sides of the scales (e). Figures b to e are of another cycad of the genus *Zamia*.

9b Shrubs or trees with needle-like leaves. The PINES. Fig. 21......
...............................PINYON PINE *Pinus edulis Eng.*

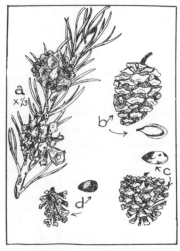

Figure 21

This tree (a) grows to a height of 50 ft. The crown is rounded and the bark reddish brown. The blueish-green leaves are about 1½ in. long and borne in bundles of 2. The nuts of this and of the three other species mentioned are prized as food. They are usually roasted. The cones are egg-shaped or globular and usually 2 in. or less in length. All 4 species are found in our southwestern states.

The SINGLELEAF PINYON (b) has yellowish green leaves, usually with but one in a bundle. It is the only one having wings on the nuts. The usual number of needles to a bundle in the MEXICAN PINYON (d) is 3 while the PARRY PINYON (c) has 4.

THE ANGIOSPERMS

10a Leaves usually parallel-veined (a); flowering parts usually in 3's (b); stem with vascular bundles scattered throughout or hollow; seeds with but one cotyledon. Fig. 22. The MONOCOTYLEDONS...11

Figure 22

10b Leaves usually net veined (a); flowering parts usually in 5's (sometimes 4's) (b); stems with vascular bundles arranged in a ring circling the pith; seeds with two cotyledons. Fig. 23. The DICO-TYLEDONS 45

Figure 23

THE MONOCOTYLEDONS

11a Flowers minute, surrounded by chaffy bracts (glumes); and grouped in spikes or spikelets. Leaves in two rows on the stem. Stems usually cylindric and almost always hollow; fruit a grain. Fig. 24. GRASS FAMILY, Gramineae.................12

Figure 24

12a Flowers and fruit borne at top of plant in spikes (a); or panicles (b). Fig. 25 18

Figure 25

12b Staminate flowers borne at top of plant in a panicle (tassel); pistillate flowers and fruit (ear) borne in axil of leaves on side of plant, enclosed in leafy husks. Fig. 26.................................

MAIZE or INDIAN CORN Zea mays L. (go to number 13 for varieties)

A heavy set solid stemmed, plant normally 3 to 15 feet high. It is unbranched except that sprouting plants (suckers) often arise from the base. The lower joints or nodes bear prop or brace roots which aid in holding the plant erect. The pistillate (female) flowers are borne in spikes arising from the side of the plant at about half its height. These spikes are surrounded by a heavy growth of modified leaves, the husks. Each flower (ovary) develops into a kernel of corn and the spike becomes an "ear." The flowers or kernels are arranged in double rows on the cob, so that an ear of corn may have from 4 to sometimes more than 20 rows of kernels (but always an even number).

Figure 26

Mature ears range from 3 to 12 inches in length and may contain 800 or more kernels which may be white, yellow, black, blue or red and are sometimes striped. Cobs are either red or white. One strand of silk arises from each flower for this is the stigma which must receive a pollen grain if the kernel is to mature. The hundreds of strands of silk run along the ear and protrude from the husks at its tip in a mass of threads, where they receive the pollen as it is carried in the air.

Corn has been greatly improved in both yield and quality by hybridizing inbred strains. Our country produced 3,451,292,000 bushels of corn in 1956.

13a The individual kernels of the ear not enclosed in a pod or husk..14

13b Each kernel enclosed in a separate pod or husk. Fig. 27. . . . .
. . . . POD CORN Zea mays var. *tunicata* St. Hil.

a, ear; b, individual kernels.

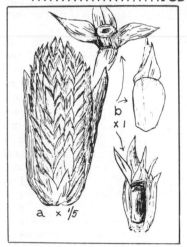

Pod, or Husk Corn as it is sometimes called, is raised as a novelty rather than for its practical value. All parts of the plant except the ears are the same as in other varieties of corn. Each kernel is enclosed separately in a husk, then the entire ear is covered with husks as in other varieties. The kernels may be flint, dent, sweet or pop corn and carry the several corn colors. Pod corn is thought to have been brought to this country from Argentina. It is supposed by some to represent a primitive ancestor of our present day corn.

Figure 27

14a Grains pop when heated (starch grains suddenly expand turning the kernel inside out). Fig. 28. . . . .
. . . . POP CORN Zea mays var. *everta* Bailey

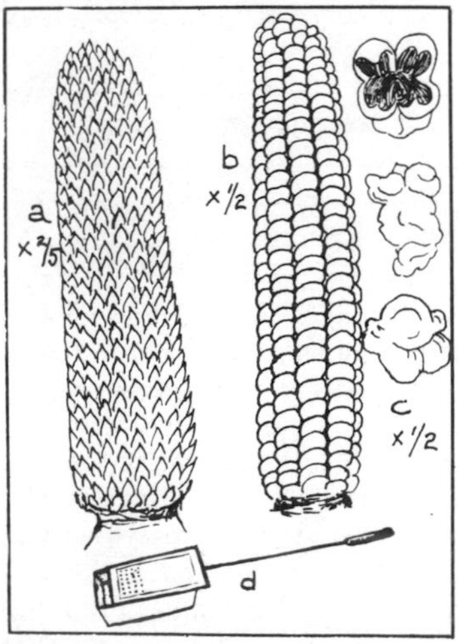

a, rice popcorn; b, pearl popcorn; c, kernels when "popped"; d, a simple corn popper.

Popcorn seems to belong with the movies, baseball games or circuses! Its importance as a food item is greater than often realized. The endosperm of the kernels is flinty throughout or nearly so. The moisture within the kernels causes them to explode when heated.

The small kernels of Rice popcorn are sharp pointed. This type is a favorite for home use. The kernels of Pearl popcorn are smooth and usually larger than the rice type. Popcorn has smaller stalks and ears than field corn. Red, yellow, white and blue colors prevail; occasionally all of these colors appearing in one ear. Ears range from 2 to 7 inches long.

Figure 28

14b Grains not popping when heated. 15

15a Kernels with no corneous (horny starch) endosperm. Grains soft.
Fig. 29............SOFT CORN *Zea mays* var. *amylacea* Bailey

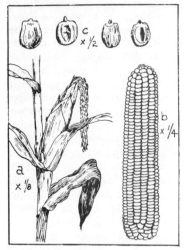

Figure 29

a, stalk with ear; b, typical ear, husked; c, kernels.

Soft corn is much the opposite of Pop corn. In the latter all of the endosperm is hard flinty (corneous) starch whereas in Soft Corn there is no corneous tissue. The kernels maintain their smooth outer surface and resemble Flint Corn. Ears are usually 8 to 10 inches long with 8 to 12 rows of kernels. In general appearance they resemble Flint Corn. It may take any of the corn colors 'except deep yellow, as corneous tissue is necessary for that color.

The ears of corn found in South American tombs are of this variety. Soft Corn is planted in South America, Mexico and our Southwestern States and is used in flour making.

15b At least a part of the endosperm of kernels, corneous..........16
16a Kernels horny and translucent throughout; more or less wrinkled
when dry. Fig. 30....SWEET CORN *Zea mays* var. *rugosa* Bonaf.

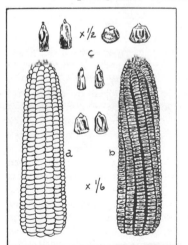

Figure 30

a, ear ready for eating; b, dry ear; c, matured dry kernels.

The leaves and green stems of the corn plants make carbohydrates by photosynthesis. This organized food is transferred through the vascular bundles of the plant in the form of sugar (glucose). When it is stored, as in the kernels it is converted into starch, since that is more stable. In sweet corn this change is but partial so that while some starch is found in the kernels, much of the contents is glucose giving it its sweet taste. The fresh unripened kernels are tightly filled and smooth, but due to shrinkage as the water dries out of the glucose the ripened kernels are much wrinkled. They are also translucent.

Sweet corn is an important food crop, sold fresh from the field or canned in great quantities. Dried sweet corn was once very common in homes and in the markets.

16b Kernels smooth; at least at their sides........................17

17a Starchy endosperm wholly enclosed by corneous endosperm; kernels small and smooth at end. Fig. 31.........................
.........FLINT or YANKEE CORN *Zea mays* var. *indurata* Bailey

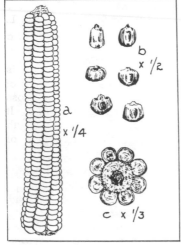

Figure 31

a, typical ear; b, kernels; c, cross section of ear showing cob with pith at center.

Flint corn, in character, stands midway between pop corn and dent corn. The ears are usually 8 to 15 inches long and comparatively slim and run to all the common colors of corn. It has a deeper shade of yellow than found in dent corn. The number of rows is smaller than in dent corn, 4 to 12.

Flint corn is raised in regions where dent corn will not mature but is being replaced in some of these by short season dent corn. It often produces several ears to a stalk and is a fairly good yielder. Columbus found a flint corn in the West Indies which has developed into the "tropical flint" and is now planted in Argentina and some European countries.

17b Kernels with starchy endosperm at top, resulting in a characteristic dent when dry. Fig. 32...................................
....................DENT CORN *Zea mays* var. *indentata* Bailey

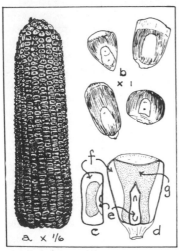

Figure 32

a, typical ear; b, kernels of different shapes; c, cross section of kernel; d, longitudinal section of kernel; e, embryo; f, flinty starch of endosperm; g, soft starch of endosperm.

This is the type of corn raised in the great corn belt of our country. There are many strains and varieties. Yellow is the most frequent color, though white varieties are common. Red and blue kernels are sometimes seen.

The practice of crossing two carefully selected inbred strains to produce hybrid seed has greatly increased the corn yield as well as making the plants much more uniform. Yields of well over 100 bushels per acre are now common. The average yield for all of Iowa in 1957 was estimated at 59 bushels per acre.

22

18a Stems hollow; except at the nodes..........................22
18b Stems solid 19
19a (b,c) Coarse branching plant with imperfect flowers and bearing hard oval shining seeds about 1/3 inch in diameter. Fig. 33...... ....JOB'S-TEARS *Coix lacryma-jobi* L.

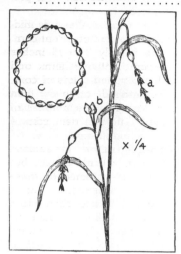

Figure 33

a, staminate flowers; b, seeds; c, a necklace made of Job's-tears.

This very interesting plant is thought by some to be an ancestor of our common corn but efforts to cross the two have been unsuccessful. It resembles the corn plant in its growth habits. It may attain a height of eight feet.

The smooth enamel-like blueish seeds are employed as ornaments and strung for beads or bracelets. A variety producing soft seeds is raised in the warmer parts of Asia for food. In our country it is only a garden curiosity. It is apparently a native of India.

19b Nodes numerous (several to each foot of stem). Seed seldom produced except in tropics. Fig. 34.................................. ....SUGAR-CANE *Saccharum officinarum* L.

Figure 34

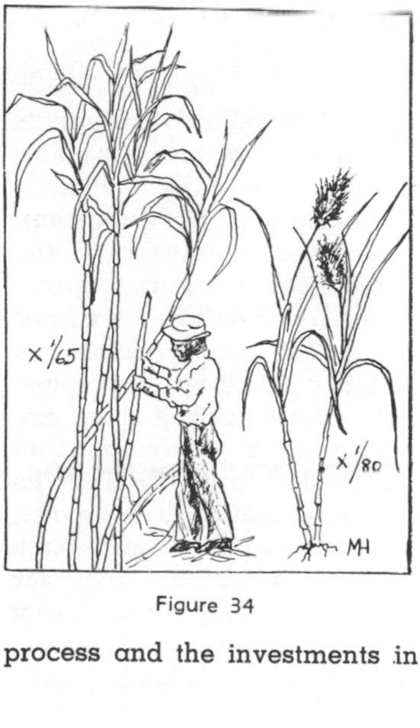

Sugar cane seems to have originated in Arabia. It has a long history and is raised throughout the warmer areas of the world. It is a heavy solid stemmed plant with the joints closer placed than in corn. It stands 8 to 15 feet high with numerous leaves two inches wide and some 3 feet long. The silky panicle at its top may be 2 feet in height. It seldom matures seed and is most frequently propagated by planting pieces of the stem. After cutting, the roots throw up vigorous suckers for the next crop so that replanting is done only once every 4 to 6 years.

The making of sugar from this plant is one of man's oldest industries. It is now a highly intricate process and the investments in raising, harvesting, and processing the plants makes it one of the world's greatest industries. Our country produced over seven million tons of sugar in 1955.

19c Some or all of the flowers perfect. The SORGHUMS.........20

20a (b,c) Pith with abundant very sweet juice; internodes long; seeds reddish-brown. Fig. 35.....................................
........SWEET SORGHUM *Sorgum vulgare* var. *saccharatum* B.

Figure 35

a, growing plant; b, head of "orange" sorghum; c, head of "amber" variety; d, seed.

Our present day sorghums are thought to have been derived from a widely scattered tropical plant sometimes raised for forage like Johnson-grass. The cultural improvements of the plant have diverged into sweet sorghums and grain sorghums. The variety *saccharatum*, here pictured, has an abundant sweet juice in its pithy stem from which Sorghum sirup is made. The plant attains a height of 8 to 15 feet.

When the plants have reached their maximum size and the seed is in the dough stage the quantity of juice and percentage of sugar are at their best. The leaves are stripped from the stalks which are then cut and the heads removed. At the mill, rollers remove the juice which is boiled down. An acre may produce 200 to 450 gallons of sirup.

20b Pith with but scanty juice; but slightly sweet or somewhat acid; internodes short; heads cylindrical. Fig. 36.....................
.....................KAFFIR *Sorgum vulgare* var. *caffrorum* B.

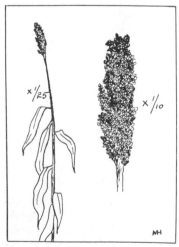

Figure 36

The grain sorghums produce a grain similar in food value to maize and can be successfully grown in semi-arid regions where the rain fall is insufficient for growing maize. The Kaffirs comprise a valuable group though they run into several strains or varieties. The heads are always erect, on plants 5 to 7 feet high. Red, white, pink and black-hull types are recognized, with the red seeming to enjoy the greatest favor. Kaffir came originally from Natal. It is known that the sorghums have been cultivated in both Africa and Asia for at least 2000 to 3000 years.

21a Fruiting head compact; 4 to 10 inches long; seeds strongly flattened. Fig. 37.............DURRA *Sorgum vulgare* var. *durra* B.

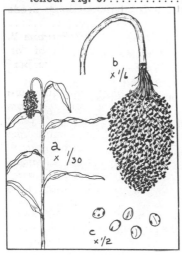

a, mature plant; b, fruiting head; c, grains.

The stems are medium to heavy, 4 to 7 feet high and ½ to 1½ inches thick; the pith is usually dry although in some varieties it has scanty juice. The panicles (fruiting heads) are compact and often hanging on a recurved stem. The seeds are decidedly flattened. The types are separated by their seed and glume colors.

In our country, Durra is raised mostly in the Southwest, having come from Northern Africa. Other varieties are raised in Northeast Africa and in India but none of these have proven suited to our climate.

Figure 37

21b Head umbel-shaped, the branches much elongated, their tips drooping; rachis short, seeds reddish. Fig. 38.......................
.........................BROOM CORN *Sorgum vulgare* Pers.

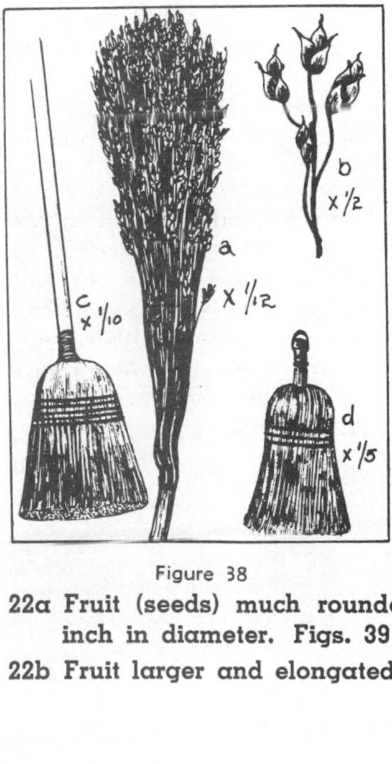

a, part of fruiting head; b, fruit (seeds); c, broom; d, whisk broom.

This plant is the basis for a substantial industry. It has been bred to produce long, brush-like panicles with tough slender branches.

The plants range up to 15 feet in height and bear panicles 10 to 28 inches in length. It is planted and cultivated much the same as other sorghums. The heads (brush) are cut from the plants near the close of the blooming period, the seeds removed, dried quickly to keep them green and tough, then bailed for the market.

Figure 38

22a Fruit (seeds) much rounded, often nearly spherical, 1/16 to 1/8 inch in diameter. Figs. 39 to 41..............The MILLETS....23

22b Fruit larger and elongated. Figs. 42 to 47....The CEREALS....25

23a Head a drooping panicle without awns; 2½ to 4 feet high. Fig. 39.
................BROOM-CORN MILLET *Panicum miliaceum* L.

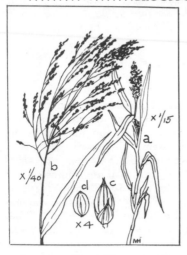

a, plant to show growth habits; b, panicle; c, spiklet bearing one seed; d, seed.

This is the true millet of the old world which has been cultivated for its seed to use as food since before our earliest history. It does well in poor soil and with scant rainfall. It is an annual attaining a height of 3 to 4 feet. Its stems and leaves are rather densely covered with hairs. The seeds are ground for flour and may be used in puddings and soups. It often plays an important role in canary bird seed.

It is a good short season plant and has been extensively raised in our northern areas.

Figure 39

23b Inflorescence a spike (sometimes compounded) with numerous bristles or awns...24

24a Globose grain opening the hull at maturity. Spike dense. Plants 3 to 8 feet tall; stems pithy. Fig. 40...........................
................PEARL MILLET *Pennisetum glaucum* R. Br.

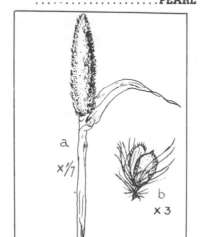

a, terminal spike; b, seed as borne in the fruiting head.

This is also known as Indian or African Millet and Cattail Millet. The plant is tall and coarse (6 to 15 feet) with large thick compact spike 6 to 14 inches long and often an inch thick. Its use in this country is mostly for forage but in the old world it has ages been an item of human food.

It yields an enormous amount of forage; may be cut two or three times per season but is difficult to handle and not very favorably regarded in this country.

Figure 40

24b Seed enclosed in hull when mature; spike rather open. Plants 2 to 5 feet tall. Fig. 41....FOXTAIL MILLETS *Setaria italica* Beauv.

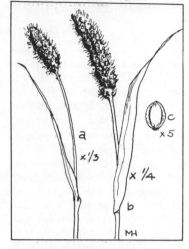

a, Hungarian millet; b, Common millet; c, seed.

When Millet is mentioned in America it is usually this plant that is in mind. It is an annual, growing from 2 to 5 feet high. The head is a compact cylindrical panicle with many short awns and very numerous nearly-spherical seeds. The seeds are usually yellow but other colors are found in some varieties. This plant is highly prolific. The seeds are used as human food in the old world, but with us this species of millet figures largely as a forage plant and for cropping purposes.

Figure 41

26a (b, c) Spikelets perfect, flattened and with but one seed. Fig. 42..
....RICE *Oryza sativa* L.

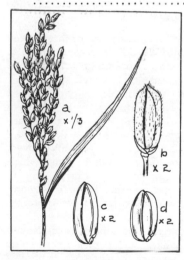

a, fruiting head; b, spikelet with one seed; c, grain of long Honduras type; d, grain of Japanese type.

This in all probability is the world's greatest food plant for more than one third of the people of the world make it their chief food. The Chinese have raised it for at least 4000 years.

Rice growing was started in the United States in 1694 along the southern Atlantic coast. Rice is normally a flood-land crop but in our country is usually sowed and cared for as the other small grain crops but is flooded by irrigation during part of its growth, then the water is drained away and binders or combines used

Figure 42

for harvesting. Upland rice is a variety that does not require flooding. The grain after threshing is still enclosed in its hull and in this form is known as "paddy rice." When the hull is removed by milling, "brown rice" results; further milling removes this coat and the grains are then put through a polishing process which yields rice as we ordinarily know it.

Puffed rice is exploded by steam with a result equivalent to popped corn.

In 1955 our country produced 53,000,000 bags of rice.

26b Spikelets unisexual, rounded and with but one flower; pistillate spikelets on the upper part of the panicle, the staminate spikelets below. Fig. 43..................WILD RICE *Zizania aquatica* L.

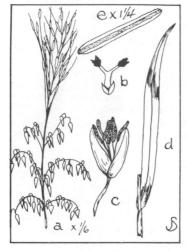

a, flowering panicle; b, pistil; c, staminate flower; d, leaf; e, mature grain.

This plant grows to a height of 9 or 10 ft. in marshy areas and is widely scattered from Canada to our gulf coast. It has been introduced into new localities to serve as food for wild water foul. The grains are cylindrical, slender and ½ in. or more in length. It has had long use with the Indians. In more recent years it has been in rather heavy demand and is highly regarded, especially to serve with wild game.

It is also known as Indian Rice and Water Oats.

Figure 43

26c Spikelets perfect, rounded and usually producing two or three seeds (rarely but one). Fig. 44.......COMMON OATS *Avena sativa* L.

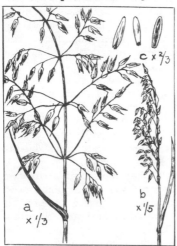

a, head of spreading oats; b, head of side-oats; c, threshed grains.

This is a highly important food crop. The plants grow 2 to 4 feet high. There are two types, spreading oats and side-oats, the former being the one most frequently raised. It is a self-pollinated plant which makes improvement fairly easy to attain and retain. There are many recent varieties which have greatly raised the average yield.

Oats (with the exception of "Naked Oats") like barley and rice retains its hull when threshed which makes it lighter in weight than wheat or rye. Our country produced 1,575,736,-000 bushels of oats in 1955.

For human food it is made into oatmeal, a steel cut granulated prod-

Figure 44

uct or into rolled oats. In making the latter the hulled grains are run through heated metal rollers producing the familiar flakes.

WILD OAT, *Avena fatua* L., is a weed and has little or no food value.

27a Each node of rachis bearing 3 one-flowered spikelets. Grain retains its hull when threshed. Fig. 45...........................
....BARLEY *Hordeum vulgare* L.

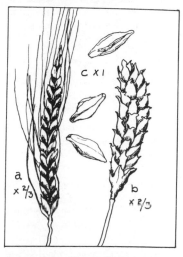

Figure 45

a, head of bearded barley; b, beardless variety; c, grain when threshed.

This is thought to be man's oldest grain crop. It likely originated in Western Asia. The plant resembles wheat but does not grow as tall. The actual kernel is much like that of wheat but is covered with the flowering glume and palea (floral parts) which make the hull. This hull constitutes some 20% or more of the total weight but adds more than that to the bulk.

There are two distinct types, two rowed and six rowed barley. Four rowed barley is a variety of the six rowed, type in which the side rows intermingle making two rows appear as one.

Barley will thrive in even colder climates than wheat or rye. It is a favorite for making malt beverages. Barley meal is much used for baking in Europe but lacks favor in America. Pearl barley is made by removing the hull and polishing the grains. It is used as a cereal and in soups. 291,589,000 bu. is a ten-year average yield for our country.

28a Spikelets uniformly 3-flowered producing 2 grains with the middle flower sterile. Glumes one-nerved and narrow. Fig. 46.........
....**RYE** *Secale cereale* L.

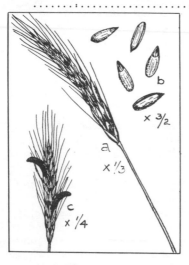

a, typical head; b, threshed grains; c, head with two Ergoted grains— a common fungus disease of rye.

Rye resembles wheat but is a taller plant and will grow in a colder climate. It is the principal grain crop of Northern Europe and parts of Asia. It has been known for some 2000 years but not as long as wheat and barley. Since it is cross-pollinated there are comparatively few varieties.

Like all the small grains, stooling or tillering greatly multiplies the yield. When a seed grain grows it does not produce just one stalk as might be supposed, but sends up several stalks each bearing a fruiting head.

Figure 46

Rye flour is much used throughout Europe and is considerably used in our country. Its food value is about the same as wheat, though it has less protein. We raise over 30 bushels of wheat for every one of rye.

28b Spikelets with 2 to 5 flowers. Glumes broader and with 3 nerves. Fig. 47............................WHEAT *Triticum aestivum* L.

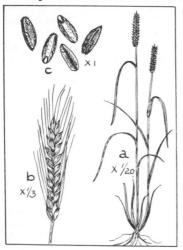

a, typical plant of beardless wheat; b, head of bearded wheat; c, wheat grains.

Wheat is a close rival to rice as the world's greatest food plant. It is an annual grass easily raised and growing in many parts of the world. The grains will average a bit shorter and noticeably plumper than rye. In some regions it is sowed in the fall and makes considerable growth before cold weather, rests during the winter then completes its growth the following year.

Spring wheat is not sowed till after winter and makes its entire growth in the one season. Fall wheat is usually the harder grain and makes the best flour. Wheat flour

Figure 47

is superior to all others for bread-making due to its quantities of gluten. Wheat is used for breakfast foods in the same way as oats—rolled wheat, cracked wheat, puffed wheat and wheat flakes. Our country produced 1,036,814,000 bushels of wheat in 1956.

29a Plants with palm-type foliage; leaves very large, one group with pinnately compound leaves, the other with palmately divided ones. . . . . PALM FAMILY Palmaceae 30

29b Plants not having large palm-like leaves 32

30a Leaves pinnate or feather-shaped. (See Figs. 49 and 50) 31

30b Leaves palmately veined and divided; fan-like. Fig. 48 . . . .
. . . . CABBAGE PALM *Sabal palmetto* Todd.

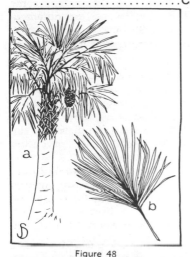

a, tree with fruit; b, leaf.

This tree is native of our southeastern states and is especially abundant in Florida. The Indians ate the berries but it is the large terminal bud from which the tree gets its name. This bud and the surrounding tissues are eaten cooked or raw. It is a highly regarded delicacy. Of course it kills the tree to remove the terminal bud so it should be used quite sparingly.

The pith of several palms of the genus *Metroxylon* of the East Indies is used to prepare sago, a starchy food.

Figure 48

31a Fruit, great globular oblong bodies borne near top of trunk. Monoecious. Fig. 49 . . . . COCONUT *Cocos nucifera* L.

a, tree with nuts; b, cross section of fruit showing nut inside; c, cross section of germinating seed.

This is one of the most widely distributed tropical trees. Its rather slender trunk attains a height of 60 to 100 feet. It has four important uses; the flower clusters when punctured secrete a sap from which a beverage "toddy" is made. Sugar is also made from this sap. The fruit consists of a single seed, a coconut, which is surrounded by a heavy fibrous covering. The fibers from this outer husk, "coir," are much used in the manufacture of mats, brushes, etc.

Figure 49

31

The coconut, which is the world's largest seed, has a woody shell lined with about a half inch layer of white "meat." The remaining interior is partly filled with a sweetened liquid, the "milk." This meat and its enclosed liquid are important food sources. The dried meat "copra" is a major source of oil.

31b Fruit, fleshy cylindric drupes one to two inches long, borne in great clusters, arising among the leaves. Dioecious. Fig. 50..............
...........................DATE PALM *Phoenix dactylifera* L.

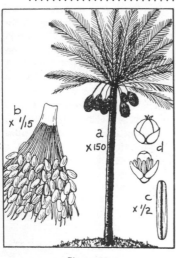

a, tree with bunches of fruit; b, single spray of fruit; c, seed; d, flowers.

The use of dried dates for food goes back many centuries. The tree seems to have originated in Africa. The trees which may reach a height of 100 feet or more are distinctly staminate or pistillate. By practicing hand pollination only a few staminate trees need to be grown to insure fruit production of several hundred pistillate trees. Dates may ripen on the tree but are usually cut green and ripened in a warm room as with bananas.

Figure 50

A Date Palm tree comes into bearing at 5 or 6 years and may continue for more than 100 years. 100 to 200 pounds of dates is an average yield per tree, though careful cultivation produces yields up to 600 pounds. There are many known varieties. Dates are grown commercially in the dryer areas of California and Arizona. Florida has the temperature needed, but too much rainfall for their successful culture.

32a Broad leaved tropical plants with flowers borne on a fleshy spadix surrounded by a spathe (as in Calla Lily).....................33

32b Not as in 32a...34

33a Plant without stem above ground. Edible parts the heavy corms from which the broad "elephant ear" leaves arise. Fig. 51......
.............................TARO *Colocasia esculenta* Schott.

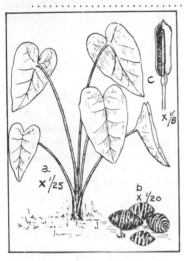

Figure 51

a, plant; b, the corms; c, flowers.

This very large-leaved plant is confined to regions of warm climate. The plant grows from a central large corm weighing up to 6 pounds and produces numerous smaller lateral tubers about the size of a hen egg or larger. The outer covering is fibrous and brown, the interior is white and starchy. These corms can be prepared for the table the same way as potatoes and make a good substitute. They have less water than potatoes. They have a pleasing nutty flavor. Dasheen is another name.

Young forced branched shoots from the corms are eaten similarly to asparagus. They are said to have a mushroom-like flavor.

A closely related species known as Elephant's Ear is often grown for ornament.

33b A climbing plant with large thick perforated leaves. Edible part the large spadix which ripens into a fleshy fruit. Fig. 52.......
.............................CERIMAN *Monstera delicosa* Liebm.

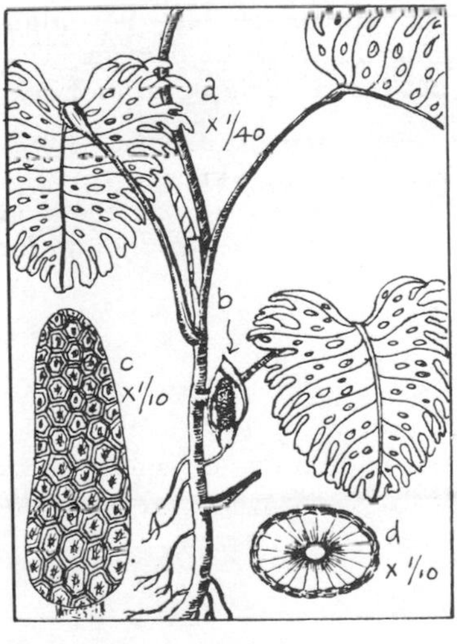

Figure 52

a, portion of plant, b, spathe (a bract) surrounding the spadix of the inflorescence; c, mature fruit; d, cross section through fruit.

This tropical American woody climber may be distinguished by its large thick leaves up to 3 feet across and which are perforated with numerous large slots and holes. Long cord-like aerial roots trail from its stem. It is abundant in Mexico and Central America and is sometimes raised in green houses in temperate regions.

The flowering spathe attains a length of 10 to 16 inches and is nearly white. It surrounds the fleshy somewhat shorter spadix which in this plant, becomes edible when ripened. The thin outer yellowish-green covering peels off readily. The fruit has a tempting fragrance and a taste not unlike mixed banana and pineapple.

34a Plants with great, stiff, fleshy leaves in basal rosettes. The leaves are usually spiny especially at the tip. Fig. 53.................
....**AGAVES** *Agave* spp.

The genus is made up of about 300 species of plants. In Mexico and other tropical lands, Agaves furnish fibers, food, fermented liquors and soap. The bases of the fleshy leaves and the flower buds are eaten. Sisal, Henequen, Maguey, Ixtle, and other fibers are made from these plants, most of which goes into the production of ropes and cords as they are usually too coarse and harsh to make good cloth.

The Century Plants (several species), which we see grown as an ornamental, belong here. They bloom in ten or more years in the tropics at which time the food contents of the great fleshy leaves is consumed in building the stately flowering

Figure 53

panicle sometimes 40 feet high and bearing hundreds of flowers. The main plant dies after maturing its seed, but others come up at its base.

34b Plants not as in 34a...**35**

35a (b, c) Plants, the fruit of which is used for food..............**44**

35b Underground parts or leaves used for food...................**36**

35c Thick young stems used for food. Older plants, tall, much divided with small, yellowish lily-like flowers and spherical fruit (red when ripe). Fig. 54..
.................GARDEN ASPARAGUS *Asparagus officinalis* L.

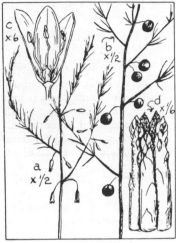

a, small branch of plant with flowers; b, branch with fruit; c, section of flower; d, "spears" as cut for market.

Asparagus over-winters as a mass of fleshy underground stems (rhizomes) at a depth of several inches. The mature plants are much branched with fine linear leaves and attain a height of 5 to 6 feet. The flowers are tiny, hanging and tulip-shaped, for this plant belongs to the Lily family. Their color is yellowish. The fruit is a berry, scarlet at maturity.

The fleshy young sprouts or "spears" are cut close to the ground when they have attained a height of 4 to 8 inches and bunched for marketing or canning. It is a native of Europe where a beverage is made from the ripe fruit and the seeds sometimes serve as a substitute for coffee.

Figure 54

36a Lily-like plants growing from true bulbs. Usually the bulbs are eaten, but sometimes the leaves............................37

36b Food source the more or less thickened true roots or rhizomes..42

37a Leaves cylindrical and hollow................................39

37b Leaves solid and grasslike.................................38

38a Leaves broad. Fig. 55.................LEEK *Allium porrum* L.

Figure 55

a, plant as eaten; b, flowering head.

This is a close relative of the common onion. Its slender elongated bulb is eaten as are also the leaves. The flavor when cooked is milder than that of the onion and distinctive. It is often used in soups. The flowers are pinkish. The plants may attain a height of 3 feet with leaves 2 inches broad. The plants are hardy and can live outside during the winter. For convenience of winter use they are usually stored in the cellar in early winter.

It seems to be of European origin.

38b Leaves narrow; bulbs composed of many bulbils. Fig. 56.......
.................................GARLIC *Allium sativum* L.

Figure 56

a, bulb; b, bulbs as frequently tied for winter; c, umbel of flowers; d, single flower; e, a "clove."

Garlic is a favorite European plant of the onion group. Its pinkish flowers grow in dense umbels on long stalks. The flowers are often intermingled with small bulbils which may be planted to raise a new crop. The plant may reach 2 feet in height. It is raised for its bulbs which are made up of 8 to 15 sections known as "cloves," separated from each other by dry scales. Seed seldom matures and the cloves are the usual means of propagation.

A closely related Wild Garlic often grows in fields and if eaten by dairy cattle gives an objectionable taste to their milk. A little garlic goes a long way. It is said the slaves who built the pyramids were fed on garlic. The project could not have been kept secret for long in that event.

**39a Bulbs very small, growing in dense clumps; leaves used for seasoning; flowers rose-colored, prominent. Fig. 57.................
.............................CHIVE Allium schoenoprasum L.**
a, single plant; b, umbel of flowers; c, a single flower.

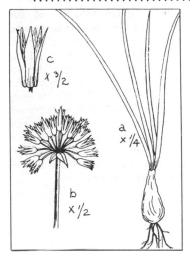

Figure 57

Chives are very hardy and once started will usually perpetuate themselves. The plants when left to themselves grow in thick masses which need to be divided and reset from time to time. They are frequently raised for ornament as the rose-purple flowers are fairly attractive, and make good border plants.

The bulbs are poorly formed so the leaves are the parts used for food in soups, salads and stews. The plants produce seed readily which permits easy large-scale raising. It is thought to be of European or Asiatic origin. Another form of the word is "Cive."

39b Bulbs larger; not in dense clumps.........................40

**40a Bulbs clustered; leaves awl-shaped, short. Fig. 58.............
.............................SHALLOT Allium ascalonicum L.**
a, bulbs; b, growing plants; c, flowering head.

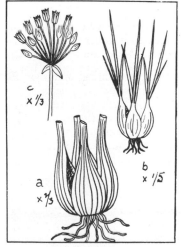

Figure 58

This plant likely originated in Asia. Its base is divided into several somewhat angular bulbs which are attached at their lower end. The leaves are short (one foot or less) and awl-like. The flowers shade from white to lilac. The flavor is more delicate than that of onions; it is used in stews, soups and pickles. Shallots are used while fresh but are more often dried and used throughout the winter. They are sometimes termed "Scallions."

Small red onions are sometimes seen in the market, being sold as shallots.

40b Leaves longer; bulbs not in clusters.........................41

41a Bulb well developed. Fig. 59.....................................
.............................COMMON ONION *Allium cepa* L.

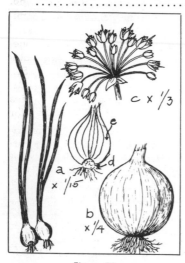

Figure 59

a, bulb and leaves; b, a mature bulb (there are many shapes); c, umbel of flowers; d, stem of bulb in cross section; e, swollen leaf (scale) for food storage.

There are literally hundreds of different species of *Allium*, many wild ones and others grown as ornamentals, but the common onion is the best known of them all. The leaves and flowering stems of this member of the lily family are cylindrical and hollow and may reach a height of three feet or more.

A variety known as "Top Onions" produces little bulbils instead of flowers on the fruiting stalk. These are saved and planted. The onion sets commonly bought in the spring are just small bulbs that have been grown from seed the preceding year.

Multiplier onions have several divisions to the bulb, each of which starts a new plant.

Field onions may yield as high as 600 bushels per acre.

41b Bulb but poorly developed at maturity. Fig. 60................
.........................WELSH ONION *Allium fistulosum* L.

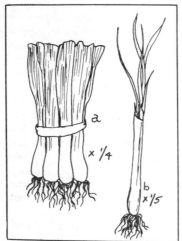

Figure 60

a, bunched for market; b, a plant as it grows.

This is another Asiatic onion which has a bulb but slightly thicker than its neck. The bulb is softer than other onions. The flowers are in dense umbels and are white with long protruding stamens. It is grown from seed.

The flavor is mild; the leaves are used for seasoning. Other names are Ciboule, Spring Onion and Rock Onion.

**42a Herbaceous vines, bearing large fleshy roots and winged seeds.
Fig. 61................CHINESE YAM** *Dioscorea batatas* **Dcne.**

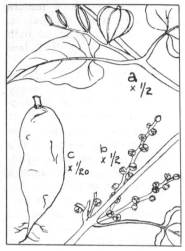

a, female vine with fruit; b, staminate vine with flowers; c, a root.

The term "Yam" is often erroneously applied to large sweet potatoes (*Ipomoea batatus*), (see Fig. 251). The true Yams are mostly tropical or belonging to the near-tropics where they are extensively used for food. The plants are strong climbing vines, of several similar species. The tuberous-like roots attain great size often weighing 30 pounds and more rarely even 100 pounds. The roots are of high food value.

Among other species than the one shown here are the YELLOW or ATTOTO YAM of the West Indies and Brazil, the CUSH-CUSH or YAMPEE—a South American species with smaller tubers and the AIR POTATO

Figure 61

(*Dioscorea bulbifera*) which bears tubers on the vine. These may attain a length of a foot and weigh several pounds. They are edible and nutritious.

42b Food derived from rhizomes (fleshy underground stems).......43

**43a Rhizomes very irregular; above ground stems unbranched, leafy, 2 to 4 feet high. Fig. 62.....................................
..................COMMON GINGER** *Zingiber officinale* **Roscoe**

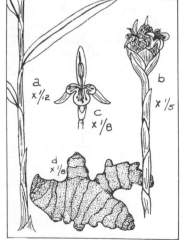

a, stalk with leaves; b, flowering spike; c, a flower; d, rhizome.

This native of the East India Islands grows from a perennial root system, but the top dies down annually. It is widely cultivated throughout the tropics. It grows to a height of 3 feet. The flowers are bright yellow marked with purple and in shape resemble some of the orchids. The rhizomes are used by cleaning and scraping to produce the ginger of the market. Young growing roots are cut into sections boiled and cured in syrup, and put into jars as a confection.

Ginger-ale, Jamaica ginger and ginger-tea are other products of this plant.

Figure 62

43b Rhizomes more regular. Stems much branched, to 6 feet high. Fig. 63.................ARROWROOT *Maranta arundinacea* **L.**

Figure 63

a, plant with roots and leaves; b, flowers.

The roots of this plant furnish arrowroot starch and one kind of tapioca. It is a native of tropical America. It attains a height of 5 or 6 feet, with leaves a foot long; its flowers are white.

The year old roots are dug, thoroughly cleaned, then beaten and rasped into a milky pulp, which is strained and put away for the starch to settle out. The starch is thoroughly dried and then canned for the market. It is used for desserts and in cooking especially for invalids and children because it is highly digestable.

44a (b, c) Edible part a collective fruit (many ovaries united to form a single fruit); leaves heavy, sword-like, spiny. Fig. 64...........
.............................PINEAPPLE *Ananas comosus* **Marr.**

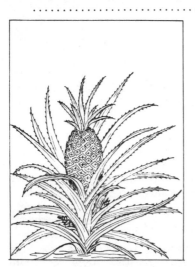

Figure 64

The pineapple is a native of tropical South America, but is now raised most largely in Cuba and Porto Rico, which supply most of the fresh fruit, and in Hawaii which produces 75% of the world's crop and features canned pineapple and pineapple juice.

Young plants are started from suckers or slips arising along the stem and at the base of the fruit of a mature plant. 8,000 to 15,000 plants are set to an acre and under favorable conditions each plant will produce a fruit weighing up to 6 or 8 pounds.

When the "pine" is young, small purplish-blue flowers appear, one in each eye of the cone. From each flower a berry develops, all packed closely together into a collective fruit.

Pineapple vinegar is sometimes made from the waste parts from peeling the fruit. The leaves yield a fiber from which the beautiful Philippine "pina" cloth is made.

44b Edible part the elongated fruit borne in large bunches. Fig. 65.
.....................BANANA *Musa paradisica* var. *sapientum* L.

Figure 65

a, plant bearing a bunch of fruit; b, the flower bracts and young fruit; c, ripe banana.

The banana is a native of the East Indies now grown in tropical America. There are several species. This species may attain a trunk diameter of a foot or more and a height of 30 feet, with leaves 2 feet wide and 9 feet long. After bearing a bunch of bananas the main shoot dies but is replaced by suckers which have grown up around it. Suckers are used to establish new plantations since seed is not produced by this species.

The flowers are borne in clusters, or "hands" of 8 to 15. Each of the 7 to 15 hands on the main stem are at first covered by a broad, usually purplish-red scale. Each flower produces one banana.

It will be noted that bananas grow with their tips up, just the reverse of the way we see them hanging in the stores.

No other agricultural crop can produce as large yields per acre as the banana. The ABACA *(Musa textilis)* has been a highly important fiber plant of the Philippines and the East Indies for cloth and cordage.

44c Flavoring extract made from fleshy bean-shaped pods. Rather fleshy climbing vine with thick leaves and fairly large flowers. Fig. 66.............COMMON VANILLA *Vanilla fragrans* Ames

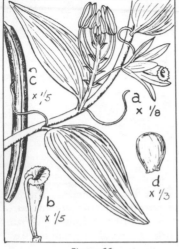

a, part of vine; b, "column" of flower; c, fruit pod; d, seed.

This climbing vine is an orchid. Its commercial worth lies in the "beans" from which vanilla extract is prepared. The flowers are greenish-yellow with lavender markings and about four inches across; the leaves attain a length of 8 inches. The pods are from 6 to 10 inches long and from ½ to ¾ inch thick.

Vanilla is a native American plant and was utilized for flavoring before the discovery of the continent. Southern Mexico produces the best vanilla though it is raised in both the West and East Indies.

Figure 66

The beans are picked from November to January and are put through an elaborate curing process, and finally tied into bunches for the market. They are soaked in grain alcohol to make the familiar Vanilla extract.

47a Stem above ground thickened into a fleshy edible part. Fig. 67...
............................**KOHLRABI** *Brassica caulorapa* Pasq.

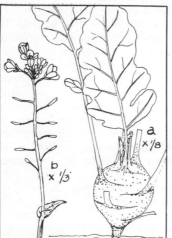

a, growing plant; b, flower and fruit stalk.

This plant resembles a turnip which forgot to keep its fleshy part under ground. It is the stem rather than the root which serves as a storage organ. In flavor it resembles the turnip but is milder.

The plants grow to a height of 10 to 18 inches; the edible swollen part is usually 2 to 4 inches in diameter and often purplish-red. The names "Stem-turnip" and "Turnip-Rooted Cabbage" are sometimes given it.

It should be grown quickly and eaten while young. It has the same insect pests as cabbage.

Flowers and seeds are produced the second year on old stocks. They are similar to those of cabbage.

Figure 67

47b Not as in 47a...48
48a Thickened fleshy roots used for food.........................49
48b Not as in 48a...52
49a Perennial plant with long irregular somewhat woody roots. Roots grated or ground for use in relishes or condiments; too hot to be eaten directly. Fig. 68.......................................
..................**HORSE-RADISH** *Armoracia lapathifolia* Gilib.

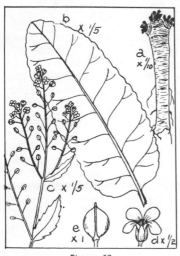

a, root as ready for the market; b, a typical leaf; c, flower and fruit branch; d, single flower; e, mature fruit.

This perennial, which reaches a height of 2 to 3 feet, is a native of Europe but is frequently found growing spontaneously as an escape. Where it is grown commercially a yield of five tons or more per acre may be had. The small lateral roots which are trimmed away before marketing the main roots, are planted to start the new crop. The root flesh is white. The flowers are white, and appear throughout much of the growing season.

Horse-radish after being prepared soon loses its flavor unless kept in tight containers.

Figure 68

49b Roots eaten raw or cooked as food.........................50
50a Plants annuals; biennial if planted late, flowers white or rose-
lilac; fruit thickened and spongy, indehiscent, few seeded. Fig. 69.
........................GARDEN RADISH *Raphanus sativus* L.

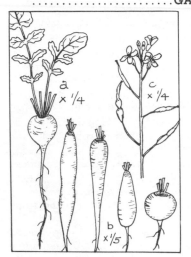

Figure 69

a, growing plant; b, some typical root shapes; c, flower and fruit stalk.

Our common radishes are annuals and need to be grown and used quickly. They soon attain maturity and flower and fruit, but are then useless for the table. There are many shapes, and sizes. Colors range from white to pink, red or purplish, often two colors appearing on the same root.

In Europe "Summer Radishes" are much used and in Asia "Winter Radishes" are in favor; both of these varieties are biennials and are larger than our spring radishes.

The root of the "Rat-tail Radish" has no food value but the soft thick pods which attain a length of a foot or more are eaten raw and used in pickels. All of these radishes are considered as belonging to the same species.

50b Biennials, flowers yellow, fruit long, many seeded (15-25), dehiscent 51
51a Leaves arising from top of swollen root; flesh white or whitish.
Fig. 70..............................TURNIP *Brassica napus* L.

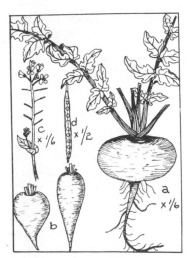

Figure 70

a, typical turnip; b, other root shapes; c, flower and fruit stalk; d, mature fruit (silique).

Turnips produce fairly large underground fleshy taproots of various shapes but usually flattened. The flesh is white and fairly fine grained. The roots are whitish with their upper parts tinged with reddish-purple. They may attain a weight of 40 pounds but are usually much smaller and only a few inches in diameter.

The roots when kept through the winter and then planted out, quickly produce tall stems bearing flowers, fruit and seeds.

Aphids are the worst insect pests of this plant.

A variety with entire leaves is known as the "strap-leaved" turnip.

51b Swollen root with short stem or neck at top from which leaves
arise; flesh yellow or orange. Fig. 71..........................
........................RUTABAGA *Brassica napobrassica* Mill.

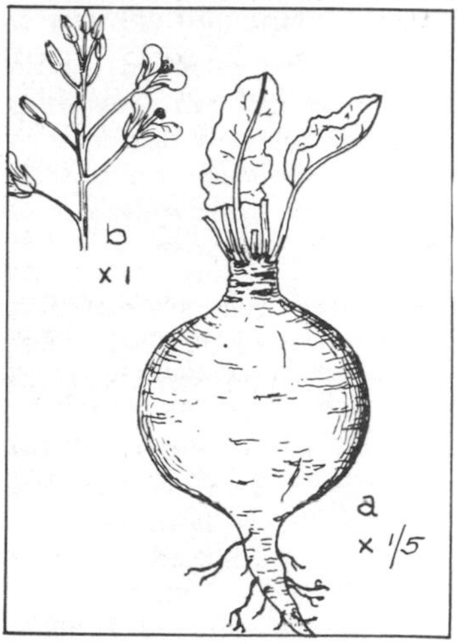

a, root and leaves; b, flowers.

Figure 71

The leaves of this plant grow to a length of 12 to 24 inches and are moderately covered with a whitish bloom giving them a blue-green shade. The plant is hardier and slower growing than its sister, the Turnip. The flowers are bright yellow and about ⅜ inch across.

Rutabagas are known also as Swede Turnips or "Swedes" and are best grown in a cool climate. They average a few pounds in weight but may become much larger.

52a The inflorescence with young buds or flowers used for food....53
52b Not as in 52a...54
53a Plant with large compact head of aborted flowers or thickened
stems. Head surrounded and overtopped by cabage like leaves;
head whitish. Fig. 72.......................................
...............CAULIFLOWER *Brassica oleracea* var. *botrytis* L.

a, top view of head.

Figure 72

This is one of several varieties of plants thought to have sprung from a wild mustard growing on the shores of western Europe. This *Brassica oleracea* in all of its varieties is one of the world's most important vegetables.

The Cauliflower plant grows and looks like cabbage, except that its head is a great mass of fasciated flower stalks and buds. The leaves grow up around this head and in field culture are often tied over it to make or keep the head white.

True Broccoli is slower growing but quite similar to Cauliflower. Sprouting or Asparagus Broccoli is the plant many know as Broccoli.

53b Heads more open and rising above the surrounding leaves; usually green with yellowish flower buds. Fig. 73..........SPROUTING or ASPARAGUS BROCCOLI *Brassica oleracea* var. *italica* Plenck.

a, head or panicle; b, buds.

This plant is characterized by its aborted, somewhat open flowering panicles. The buds and flowers are more apparent than in cauliflower. This "head" is cut while quite green and before the buds open.

All of the plants of this species are grown from seeds in green houses or special seed beds and when a few inches high are transplanted to field or garden. They are biennials and when kept alive into the second year produce flowers and seed. The production of vegetable seeds is a specialized business. The seeds of these cabbage-like plants are mostly grown in California.

Figure 73

54a Both seeds and leaves used for food.........................55

54b Leaves of plant (sometimes in compact heads) used for food....56

55a Fruit (pods) ½ to 1 inch long; held close to stem when ripe, seeds dark colored; stem leaves usually hairy. Fig. 74...............
.........................BLACK MUSTARD *Brassica nigra* Koch.

a, flowers and fruit on branch; b, fruit (silique).

This is a much branched annual, usually with stiff hairs. It grows to a height of 3 to 10 ft. The flowers are small and bright yellow. The fruit is short, usually less than one inch and very abundant.

The basal leaves of young plants are used for greens. The seeds are ground to make table mustard.

This plant is of European origin but has been scattered world-wide and is a bad weed, often growing abundantly in small grain fields and other places where it is not wanted.

Figure 74

46

55b Fruit 1½ to 2½ inches long, spreading when ripe: seeds light yellow, stem and leaves often smooth. Fig. 75....................
.......................LEAF MUSTARD *Brassica juncea* Coss.

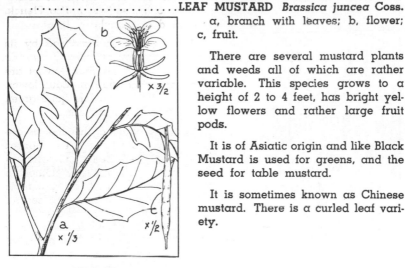

a, branch with leaves; b, flower; c, fruit.

There are several mustard plants and weeds all of which are rather variable. This species grows to a height of 2 to 4 feet, has bright yellow flowers and rather large fruit pods.

It is of Asiatic origin and like Black Mustard is used for greens, and the seed for table mustard.

It is sometimes known as Chinese mustard. There is a curled leaf variety.

Figure 75

56a Leaves closely appressed forming one or more heads..........57
56b Leaves not forming heads....................................58
57a (b,c) One single large somewhat-spherical head terminating the stem, surrounded by the earlier leaves. Fig 76................
....................CABBAGE *Brassica oleracea* var. *capitata* L.

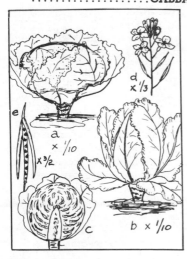

a & b, cabbage heads of two common types; c, longitudinal section through head; d, flowers; e, fruit.

Next to potatoes, cabbage is likely the most largely used vegetable. It supplies the much needed minerals, vitamins and bulk at a minimum of cost.

The plant has stored quantities of foods in the head to provide for quick growth of the flowering and fruiting parts, early the second season. Man comes in and uses these foods stored in the compactly grown fleshy leaves for his own use.

Cabbage does best when the weather is cool. There are many strains and varieties of shape and color. In Savoy cabbage the leaves are much wrinkled and blistered.

Figure 76

57b One single large cylindrical head terminating the stem. Fig. 77.
........**PE-TSAI or CELERY CABBAGE** *Brassica pekinensis* **Rupr.**

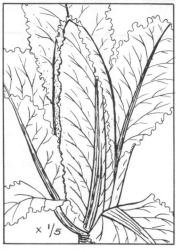

Figure 77

Chinese or "celery cabbage" is an old Chinese food plant now widely used in our country. It has a milder flavor than cabbage and is a favorite for salads and greens. The heads are elongate and slim with the inner parts bleached and will average a foot or more in length. The flowers are light yellow and the fruit rather short and heavy.

Other East Asia plants of similar nature are PAK-CHOI *(Brassica chinensis* L.) and FALSE PAK-CHOI *(Brassica parachinensis* Bailey) but neither of these are so frequently seen with us. They have less compact heads and find use in salads or as pot-herbs.

57c Many smaller heads growing along the side of the stem in the axils of the leaves. Fig. 78.....................................
...**BRUSSELS SPROUTS** *Brassica oleracea* **var.** *gemmifera* **Zenker.**

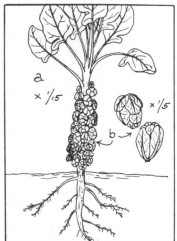

Figure 78

a, plant as grown; b, individual heads.

Scatter a lot of tiny cabbage heads along an erect stem and you have Brussels Sprouts as it is grown. The plants are raised and treated much like cabbage. The heads or "sprouts" are botanically, axillary buds which develop in the axils of the lateral leaves. When the sprouts are partly grown the leaves are removed.

The plant has been grown in Belgium (hence the name) for nearly a thousand years. The flavor is mild and in much favor. An average plant should produce about a quart of sprouts. The sprouts are ready to pick in the fall and the plant will produce flowers, fruit and seed the second season if kept indoors or protected from severe weather.

58a Fruit dehiscent (splitting open when ripe), used for salads, greens, etc. **59**

58b Fruit indehiscent, one seeded. Fleshy perennial with cabbage like leaves. Fig. 79.................SEA-KALE *Crambe maritima* **L.**

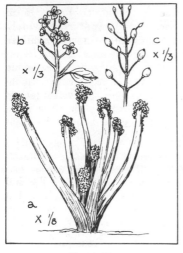

a, shoots as gathered and eaten; b, tip of flowering branch; c, fruit.

This large leaved plant attains a height of 3 feet and an age of 10 to 12 years. It grows along the west coast of Europe. The leaves are bluish green and very large, often 2 feet or more in length. They are notched and lobed more than cabbage leaves which they otherwise resemble.

It is the fleshy young blanched shoots which are eaten in much the same way as Asparagus. The plants are usually covered with light-tight receptacles to promote the maximum growth and to blanch the shoots.

The flowers are white and the fruit one seeded.

Figure 79

59a Fruit elongated **60**

59b Fruit as broad as long. Flowers white, very small. Stems and leaves glabrous and glaucous. Fig. 80........................
.........................**GARDEN CRESS** *Lepidium sativum* **L.**

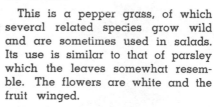
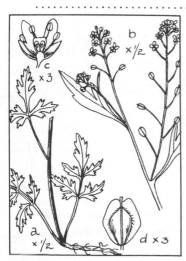

a, basal part of plant; b, flowering and fruiting shoot; c, section of flower; d, fruit.

This is a pepper grass, of which several related species grow wild and are sometimes used in salads. Its use is similar to that of parsley which the leaves somewhat resemble. The flowers are white and the fruit winged.

It is an annual raised from seed and does best in early spring and late fall. It is a native of Western Asia. As with parsley, there are curled leaf varieties which may prove more attractive but taste the same.

Figure 80

60a Rather heavy glabrous plants; flowers yellow.................61

60b Creeping or floating in water; leaves much cut; flowers large, white. Fig. 81...TRUE WATER-CRESS *Nasturtium officinale* **R. Br.**

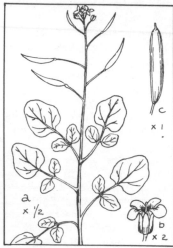

Figure 81

a, branch of plant with flower and fruit; b, flower; c, fruit.

This trailing, prostrate plant grows in cold water or mud, and having been started, usually develops spontaneously. It is valued in salads and for garnishing, not only for its flavor but also because it is very tender and brittle.

Its native home is Europe but is widely scattered because of its hardiness. The flowers are white and the fruit long stemmed. The branches take root readily when put in water or mud.

BITTER-CRESS *Cardamine pratensis* L. with white to rose-purple flowers is sometimes similarly used.

**61a Various "headless cabbage" plants. Some varieties have very much curled leaves. Fig. 82.....................................
.........KALES, BORECOLE** *Brassica oleracea* **var.** *acephala* **DC.**

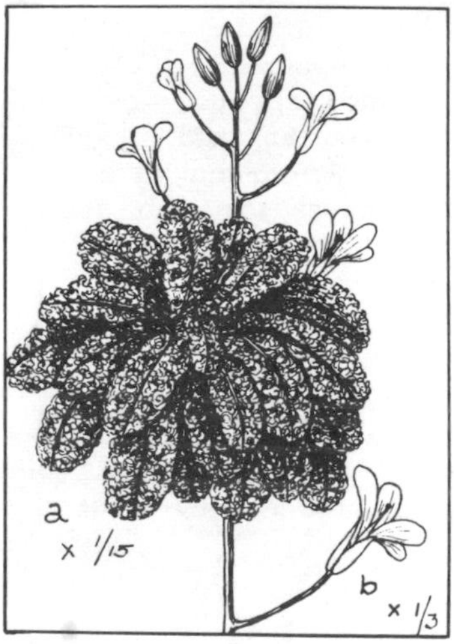

a, typical plant (curled variety); b, flowering branch.

This is one of the "cabbage plants" again, but this variety,—which runs to several strains and uses—has no modified parts. The entire plant is cut for the market although for home use, a few leaves are sometimes removed and the plant left to grow.

Collards, Tree Kales and Cow Kales belong here. They are all biennials. The curled-leaf strains seem to be most highly favored.

Figure 82

61b Dark green, thick growing, early blooming. Often abundant in fields as an escape. Fig. 83 ....
.............WINTER WATER-CRESS *Barbarea vulgaris* R. Br.

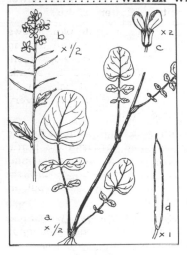

a, branch of plant; b, flowering and fruiting branch; c, flower; d, fruit.

This European plant has become a common roadside and field weed with us. Its quick growth and brilliant yellow flowers makes it conspicuous in early spring. It reaches a height of nearly 2 feet and is often a perennial. It is often known as Yellow Rocket.

Barbarea verna Asch is also known as Early Winter-Cress. It is somewhat smaller in its growing habits.

Several other members of the mustard family find occasional food uses. The family is a large one with

Figure 83

around 2,000 species known by botanists. A sharp peppery flavor is common with these plants which makes many of them desirable for use in salads.

62a Fleshy fruit-bearing trees, shrubs and perennial plants with regular 5 petaled flowers, usually showy; stamens numerous, borne on a collar-like ring. See Figs. 87-113 ROSE FAMILY 63

62b Not as above 84

63a (b,c) Plants producing aggregate fruits (few, to many fruit units arising from one flower and united into one fruit). Fig. 84 64

Figure 84

63b Plants producing stone (drupe) fruits (fleshy fruit with single stone covered "seed" near center). Fig. 85 73

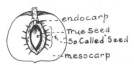

Figure 85

63c Plants producing pome fruits (fleshy fruits with usually five divisioned woody or papery "core" containing the several seeds). Fig. 86 80

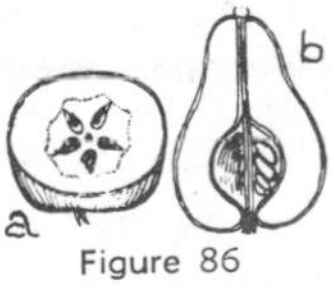

Figure 86

64a Fruit a collection of a few, to many small drupes (each "seed" with a separate flesh and skin covering) shrubs or low vines ... 65

51

64b Fruit with small hard "seeds" (really achenes) scattered over the surface of a fleshy receptacle; fruit red when ripe. Plants with very short woody stems spreading by elongated runners. Fig. 87. ....**STRAWBERRY** *Fragaria ananassa* Duchnesne

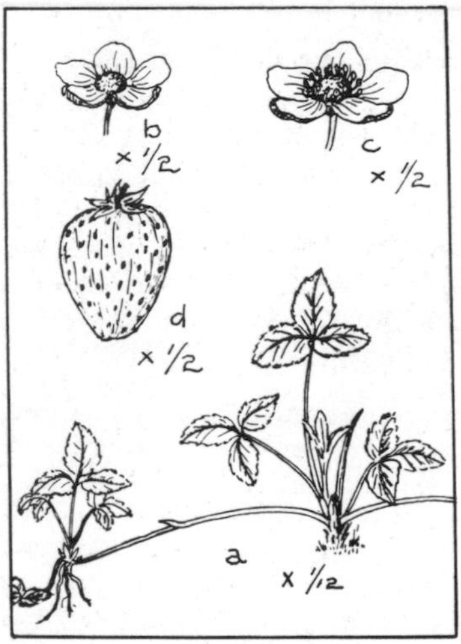

a, small plant with runner; b, flower with few stamens; c, flower with many stamens; d, fruit.

This is one of our choicest fruits, and structurally different from all others. It is a perennial herb with very short woody stems and trifoliate leaves. The flowers are white. On some varieties but few if any stamens are produced. The flowers of other varieties are perfect and have large numbers of stamens. The varieties which produce few stamens must be grown along side of some perfect-flowered variety that blooms at the same time so that pollination may be sufficiently completed to insure a good crop.

Several species of wild strawberries are known, some of which are cultivated, resulting in many hybrids.

Figure 87

The Everbearing strawberries are derived from *Fragaria vesca* L., the leaves of which are somewhat silky beneath.

65a When a ripe fruit is picked the receptacle remains on the plant. Fig. 89d. **RASPBERRIES**.......................................66

65b When a ripe fruit is picked the receptacle is detached from the plant and is a part of the "berry." **BLACKBERRIES**, etc.......68

66a Flowers small, whitish, about ½ inch across..................67

**66b Flowers 1 inch across in groups of 1-4, rose or purplish; fruit salmon to wine red. Fig. 88.....................................
.....................SALMONBERRY *Rubus spectabilis* Pursh.**

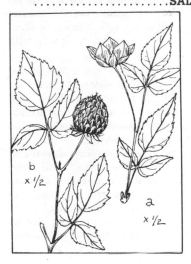

a, branch with flower; b, with fruit.

The Salmonberry is a native of the Rocky Mountain region and while edible and sometimes planted is not important as a food plant. It is a strong growing bush with but few thorns. The flowers are fully an inch in diameter and colored with different shades of rose, making it an attractive plant. The flowers are in groups of 1 to 4. The fruit, ½ to ¾ inch in diameter, is salmon to rose-red.

In flower and fruit (but not in its foliage) the Salmonberry somewhat resembles the Flowering Raspberry of our eastern mountains and is sometimes grown as an ornamental.

Figure 88

**67a Fruit purplish black when mature; glaucous canes 3-5 feet high, recurving and taking root at tip thus starting new plants. Fig. 89.
.....................BLACK RASPBERRY *Rubus occidentalis* L.**

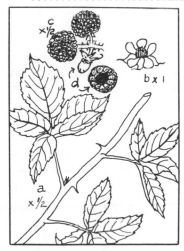

a, stem with leaves and thorns; b, flower; c, fruit; d, fruit removed with receptacle remaining on the plant.

This plant, sometimes known as the Thimble-berry reaches a height of 5 or 6 feet, but the much longer "canes" bend over and take root at their tips, by which means the plant is propogated. The canes are purplish-red and thickly covered in part with a white bloom. The flowers are greenish-white and rather inconspicuous.

Many cultivated varieties and hybrids of raspberries are known, but most of the black fruited ones have had their origin in this species which is native to much of the eastern half of our country.

Figure 89

67b Fruit red when ripe, canes not rooting at tips. Fig. 90..........
.............................**RED RASPBERRY** *Rubus idaeus* **L.**

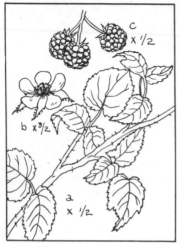

Figure 90

a, stem and leaves; b, flower; c, fruit.

This species is of European origin, though it is now more widely raised and is hardier than our black raspberries. The canes are light colored and do not take root at their tips. Multiplication is by sprouts or suckers arising at the base of the plants. The flowers are small and white. The fruit is larger and softer than that of the blackcaps. There are many varieties in cultivation.

The PURPLE RASPBERRIES or "Purple-Canes" are hybrids of the Red Raspberry and the Black Raspberry. The canes of all raspberries are biennials, coming up and growing vigorously one season, to produce fruit and die the next year. The root system is perennial and lives on.

68a Plants prostrate or creeping; rooting at tips or nodes or both. The DEWBERRIES **69**

68b Plants erect or arched, multiplying mainly by suckers though in some cases rooting at tips. The BLACKBERRIES...............**72**

69a Main stems pruinose (covered with white powdery bloom); at first ascending but becoming prostrate; stems circular in cross section with thorns scattered...**70**

69b Main stems without powdery bloom; seldom at all ascending; stems angled with most of the thorns on the ridges. Flowers perfect **71**

70a Fruit black, sweet; leaves of new canes of three leaflets or sometimes simple; flowers often imperfect. Fig. 91 . . . .
. . . . WESTERN DEWBERRY *Rubus ursinus* C. & S.
a, leaves and flower; b, fruit.

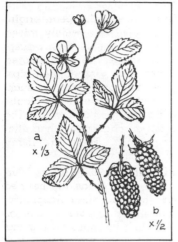

This is a native of our Pacific
coast area. The flowers are about
1 inch across and white. The fruit
when ripe is black, though white
or red fruited plants sometimes occur. The canes stand erect at first
but presently trail on the ground.
Dewberries are usually a week or
two earlier in ripening than blackberries. Where raised commercially
they are usually supported on wires.

Figure 91

70b Fruit red, sour; leaves of new canes with 3 or 5 leaflets; flowers perfect. Fig. 92 . . . . LOGANBERRY *Rubus loganobaccus* Bailey

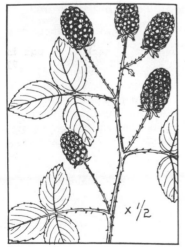

This berry which is also known
as "Phenomenal" is raised extensively on our West Coast. The flowers
are white and showy, being 1½ to 2
inches across. The fruit is elongate
and dark red.

The canes root at the tips. These
young plants are set out in rows
and the long flexible canes supported on wires. The crop is canned
in large quantities for the market.

It has been often cited as a hybrid between the Red Raspberry and
a blackberry but now seems to be
a mutant variety of the Western
Dewberry.

Figure 92

**71a Leaflets on new canes usually narrow and small; canes often brist-
ly as well as prickly. Fig. 93.......................................
.................SOUTHERN DEWBERRY *Rubus trivialis* Michx.**

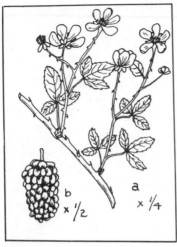

Figure 93

a, section of vine; b, mature fruit.
The stems of most dewberries are
too flexible to stand unsupported and
are trailing in habit. This one is
native from Virginia through Florida
to Texas. It has a tendency to be
evergreen.

The leaves are 3 to 5 foliate; the
flowers are about 1 inch across and
white. It is the progenitor of several
varieties valued by berry raisers.

Dewberries usually ripen earlier
than blackberries. When raised commercially they are often supported
on wire trellises or tied to stakes.
The stems are biennials, the same
as with the raspberries.

**71b Leaflets on new canes large and broad; canes with small and
weak prickles, scarcely hooked; no bristles; leaflet, broadest near
base. Fig. 94.....EASTERN DEWBERRY *Rubus flagellaris* Willd.**

Figure 94

a, part of vine; b, mature fruit.

This berry ranges throughout the
East from Canada to the Gulf. Three
leaflets are usual, though five are
sometimes seen. The flowers are
supported on long pedicels; they are
about 1 inch across and white. The
calyx lobes are unusually large as
are also the druplets composing the
shining black fruit. The large, popular Lucretia dewberry (var. *roribac-
cus*) is derived from this species.
Then there is a thornless variety,
geophilus.

72a Inflorescence long, without interspersed leaves and with gland tipped hairs. Fig. 95...
..........**MOUNTAIN BLACKBERRY** *Rubus allegheniensis* Porter.

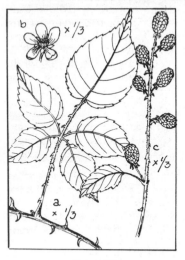

Figure 95

a, stem and leaf; b, flower; c, fruit.

This is perhaps our best known wild and cultivated blackberry. It ranges from our eastern mountains to the Middle West and is the source of several named varieties, commonly raised and marketed.

The canes of this species attain a height of 10 feet or more and are covered with vicious hooked prickles. The leaves are compound with 3 to 5 leaflets, and are pubescent on their lower surface.

Blackberries n e e d considerable moisture and a fairly cool climate. They do not do well in the South if in dry regions. When this species grows in dry open patches it may be so short and small that it might not be recognized as this same species.

72b Inflorescence short and leafy; few if any glandular hairs; leaflets on fruiting stalks narrow, evenly toothed. Fig. 96..............
............**EARLY HARVEST BLACKBERRY** *Rubus argutus* Link.

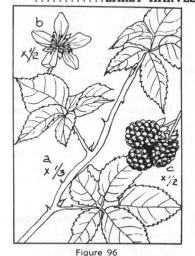

Figure 96

a, stem and leaves; b, flower; c, fruit.

This species may attain a height of five feet and has numerous prickles planted on the angles of the stem and on the petioles. Leaves with three and five leaflets. Fruit with but few seeds.

There are other native species of blackberries and among the cultivated varieties, many named forms. Some are man-made species produced by hybridizing two different species to get a wholly new plant. Some of these are patented.

73a Fruit velvety (covered with pubescence); flowers and fruit sessile or practically so; flowers large, solitary, pink, appearing ahead of foliage 74

73b Fruit smooth (glabrous) **76**
74a Flowers pale pink, stone flattened smooth except at margin; leaves
broad, abruptly sharp pointed. Fig. 97.........................
.....................COMMON APRICOT *Prunus armeniaca* L.

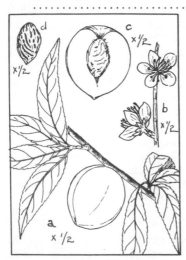

a, branch with leaves and fruit; b, flower.

This comes closest to the Peach of any of our fruits, and grows under somewhat similar conditions. The stone is much flattened and is not furred as with the peach. The flowers are ¾ to 1 inch across, pinkish to nearly white and appear very early. The fruit is yellow or reddish, somewhat flattened and breaks free from the stone.

The COMMON APRICOT originated in China, though it was long thought to have come from Armenia as the species name would indicate. The BLACK APRICOT and the JAPANESE APRICOT are used more as ornamentals than for their fruit. California produces more than 90% of our apricots.

Figure 97

74b Flowers darker, pink to reddish; stone furrowed and pitted....**75**
75a Flesh of fruit soft and juicy when ripe; young leaves sharply serrate; young twigs red on one side—green on the other. Fig. 98.
...............................PEACH *Prunus persica* Batsch.

a, branch with leaves and fruit; b, flowers; c, longitudinal section of peach; d, "seed."

Again the species name would mislead us. The peach, one of our most valued fruit crops, originated in China and not in Persia as sometimes stated. The leaves are 5 to 9 inches long and the bright pink flowers may be up to 2 inches across. The fruit which is from 1 to over 3 inches in diameter is covered with fuzz.

There are several forms grown as ornaments for their double flowers, red foliage, etc.

The NECTARINE var. *nectarina* is smooth skinned and somewhat plum like.

Figure 98

58

The FLAT PEACH, (sometimes "Saucer Peach") var. *compressa* is very much flattened at its ends.

75b Flesh hard, not eaten, splitting to the stone when mature, stone a commercial "nut." Fig. 99 ....
.........................**ALMONDS** *Prunus amygdalus* **Stokes**

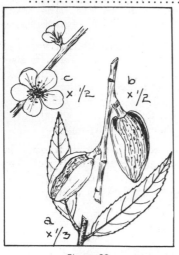

Figure 99

a, leaves; b, fruit; c, flowers.

This plant is peach-like but the scarcely fleshy outer covering of the fruit splits and is discarded for it is the stone or "nut" which is valued, the seed within being eaten. The trees are 8 to 15 feet high; the leaves 3-4 inches long, the pink flowers up to 1½ inches across and the fruit about 1½ inches long.

This tree seems to have originated in Western Asia. Bitter Almonds are a variety of this same tree. Prussic acid and other extracts are made from the bitter kernels.

The "FLOWERING ALMOND" grown for its Spring flowers is an entirely different plant, though it belongs to this same genus.

76a Stone oval, flattened; smooth except for marginal projection. PLUMS **77**
76b Stone globular, smooth. CHERRIES..........................**79**
77a (b,c) Leaves broad, reticulated, usually pubescent beneath; young twigs and fruit stems pubescent. Fig. 100......................
............**COMMON** or **EUROPEAN PLUM** *Prunus domestica* **L.**

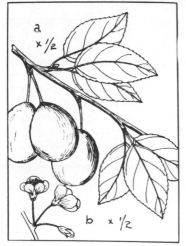

Figure 100

a, fruiting branch; b, flowers.

This tree has dull-green leaves 2-4 inches long, the flowers are white or creamy, the fruit is variable but usually bluish-purple, and about 1½ inches long. Our lowly prune is the dried fruit of this tree. They are allowed to fully ripen and drop from the tree. They are then picked up, sterilized in a lye solution and dried.

Another species, *Prunus insititia* L. with small shining dark green leaves and deep blue fruit about an inch or less in length is the common DAMSON PLUM.

77b Leaves relatively long, not reticulated, glabrous beneath except on veins, finely serrate. Fig. 101.....................
.......................JAPANESE PLUM *Prunus salicina* Lindl.

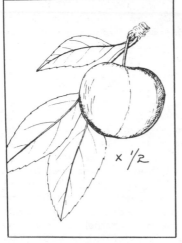

The twigs of these rather small trees are smooth, shining and usually rather light colored. The white flowers are from ½ to ¾ inch across.

There are many named varieties and the fruit varies widely in size, shape and color. There are no blue-purples however. The plant originated in China. They are quite hardy with us and seem to thrive even better than our native plums.

Brown-rot is a serious fungus disease which may take heavy toll. The Plum Curculio is likely the worst insect pest.

Figure 101

77c Leaves coarsely serrate; young twigs usually smooth; fruit yellow or red (no blue-purples). Figs. 102-104 AMERICAN PLUMS....78

78a (b,c) Trees to 20 or 30 feet, usually with thorns; flowers nearly 1 inch across; branches glabrous. Fig. 102.....................
.......................WILD PLUM *Prunus americana* Marsh.

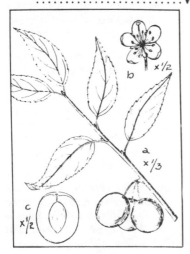

a, fruit bearing branch; b, flower; c, section through plum.

This thorny tree reaches a height of 20 to 30 feet. It is a native of the eastern part of our country. The flowers are about 1 inch across. The fruit in the wild state is usually small and hard. Varieties have been selected and grown with plums more than 1 inch long and of excellent flavor. The fruit color is yellow or red, with yellow pulp. Many named varieties are known and sold by the nurseries. Other species of "wild" plums occur throughout our country.

Figure 102

78b Much branched tree to 20 feet with zig-zag reddish branches; flowers 1/3 inch across, white, before leaves. Fig. 103..............
..................CHICKASAW PLUM *Prunus angustifolia* Marsh.

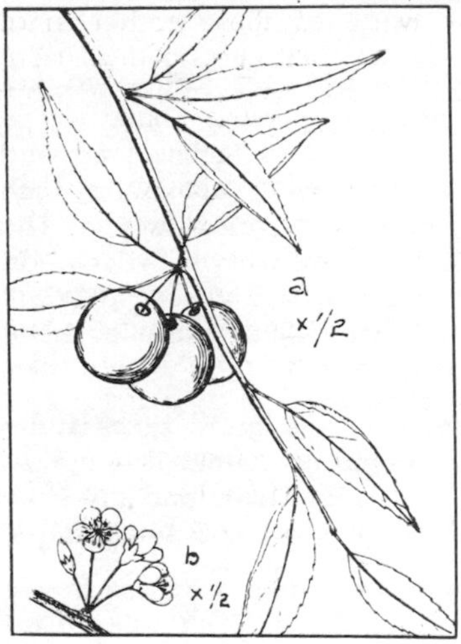

a, fruiting twig; b, flowers.

In its wild state this hardy tree bears red or yellow fruit only about ½ inch through. It may reach a height of 20 feet but is sometimes only a bush. The small white flowers are only 1/3 inch across.

A variety *watsoni* known as the SAND PLUM is a bush of 3 to 6 feet and grows in the more arid West and Southwest.

A number of valuable named varieties have been derived from this and other native plums. Their adjustment to our soils and climate make for very sturdy and profitable trees when they have been improved by breeding and selection.

Figure 103

78c Flowers ½ inch across, leaf petioles with two glands. Fig. 104....
..................WILD-GOOSE-PLUM *Prunus hortulana* Bailey

a, fruit bearing twig; b, flowers.

This is a small tree with thin bark and spreading branches. The leaves are 4-6 inches long and usually have two glands on the petiole. The flowers appear before the leaves and are about ½ inch across and white. The fruit is red with practically no bloom; flesh yellow. It is a native of the Middle West.

*   *   *

Here and there are other native plums that are gathered and eaten. Some of these have been cultivated and improved. It should not be understood that this at all concludes the list of edible plums.

Figure 104

79a Leaves comparatively long, point tapering, soft; fruit yellow or red, sweet. Fig. 105..........SWEET CHERRY *Prunus avium* L.

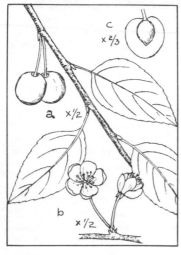

Figure 105

a, twig with fruit; b, flowers; c, cherry with stone.

This tree becomes large and tall with smooth peeling bark. The leaves are 4 to 10 inches long and flowers are white, about an inch across and hang rather limply. The fruit is solid with sweet flesh. In color it ranges from yellow to bright and dark red. Some varieties have heart-shaped fruit.

Sweet Cherries grow successfully on the Pacific coast and in the East along the Great Lakes and the Hudson River. It is of European origin.

Brown-rot sometimes causes heavy loss, while Cherry Fruit Flies, Curculio, Pear Slug and several scale insects need rather constant attention.

79b Leaves short and wider than in 79a, abruptly pointed crisp; fruit bright or dark red, sour. Fig. 106..SOUR CHERRY *Prunus cerasus* L.

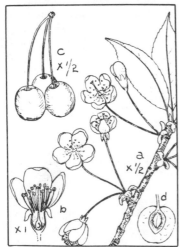

Figure 106

a, leaves and flowers; b, section of flower; c, cherries; d, fruit showing stone.

This is our common cultivated cherry which is widely distributed. The trees are broad topped, and comparatively small. The leaves are 3-4 inches long, stiff and shining. The flowers appear with the first leaves; they are white and about 1 inch across. The fruit is globular in outline, as is also its stone. Fruit colors are various shades of red.

While the per acre yield is not as large as that of Sweet Cherries this species has a much wider range and greater importance. It is sometimes known as "Pie Cherry."

80a (b,c) Core of fruit of 5 bony carpels which are exposed at tip of fruit. Fruit solitary without a pedicel. Fig. 107..................
......................................MEDLAR *Mespilus germanica* L.

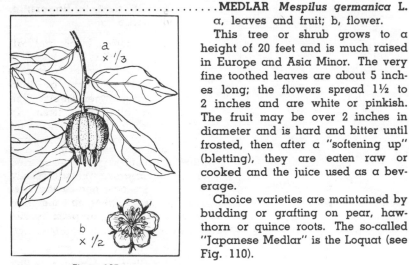

a, leaves and fruit; b, flower.

This tree or shrub grows to a height of 20 feet and is much raised in Europe and Asia Minor. The very fine toothed leaves are about 5 inches long; the flowers spread 1½ to 2 inches and are white or pinkish. The fruit may be over 2 inches in diameter and is hard and bitter until frosted, then after a "softening up" (bletting), they are eaten raw or cooked and the juice used as a beverage.

Choice varieties are maintained by budding or grafting on pear, hawthorn or quince roots. The so-called "Japanese Medlar" is the Loquat (see Fig. 110).

Figure 107

80b Fruit a small pome, (a) with 1-5 bony carpels, (b) with but one seed in each. HAWTHORNS Fig. 108..............*Crataegus* spp.

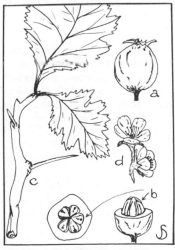

Many species of Hawthorns have been listed for our country. Some are shrubs while others are trees sometimes attaining a height of 30 feet or more. They bear a profusion of white flowers (d); the fruit varies in size with the different species but is usually some shade of red. The fruit of some species yields a good lot of juice from which beautiful and tasteful jellies can be made. Most of the species bear long sharp thorns (c).

Figure 108

80c Core of fruit parchment-like or papery; each cell 1 — several seeded 81

81a (b,c) Flowers in umbels appearing with the leaves. Fruit glabrous 82

81b Flowers and fruit solitary on ends of leafy stems; fruit greenish yellow when ripe, firm, fuzzy. Fig. 109...........................
.................................QUINCE *Cydonia oblonga* **Mill.**

a, flower and foliage; b, fruit.

This is the "true" quince. It originated in Asia and grows as a poorly formed tree or a shrub 10 to 20 feet high. The large flowers are white or tinged with pink, and have five styles and about 20 stamens. The globular or pear-shaped fruit which is borne on the end of a twig may reach a diameter of 4 inches and is yellow or greenish yellow when ripe and highly fragrant. The fruit keeps poorly; it is used for butters and preserves and is so strong flavored that a mixture of half or more of apples not only cheapens but improves the preserves.

Figure 109

THE JAPANESE QUINCE, *(Chaenomeles lagenaria)* an ornamental shrub, with brilliant red flowers, oc-
·casionally bears fruit. The CHINESE QUINCE *(Chaenomeles sinensis)* is planted in a limited way. Its fruit is large, often 6 or 7 inches long.

81c Flowers white, in terminal panicles. Evergreen shrub or tree. Fig.
110 ....LOQUAT *Eriobotrya japonica* **Lindl.**

This evergreen shrub or tree attains a height of some 20 feet and has been introduced from China and Japan into our southern areas. The small branches are covered with rusty hairs; the flowers are white and spread ½ to ¾ inch. The down-covered fruit may be globular or pear-shaped, yellow or orange and up to 3 inches long. It is juicy when ripe but has several large seeds. It is eaten raw or made into jellies or preserves.

It is sometimes called the Japanese Medlar or Japan Plum. It is being improved and new varieties produced by breeding and selection.

Figure 110

82a Flowers pink or rose occasionaly white; calyx tube open; leaves dull; no stone cells in flesh...................................83

82b Flowers white, calyx tube closed; leaves shining; fruit usually "pear-shaped" flesh often contains gritty stone cells. Fig. 111.... ....**PEAR** *Pyrus communis* L.

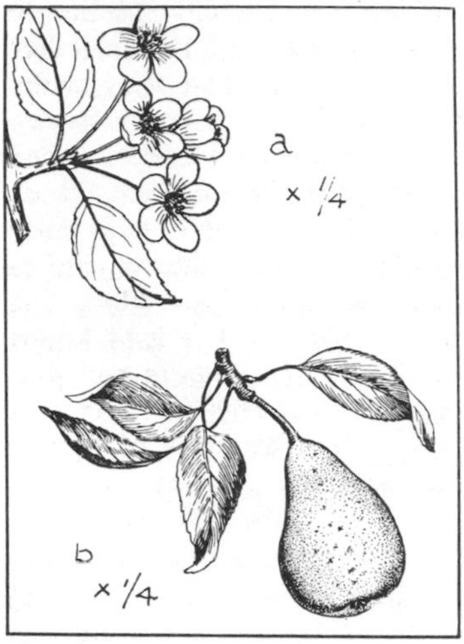

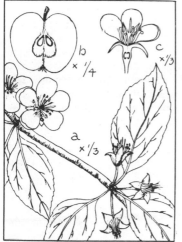

a, flowers and foliage; b, fruit.

This tree of European origin, has a long history and is grown rather world wide. The trees become large and old. The leaves are usually smooth and shining and almost black when dead. The flowers are an inch or more across and faintly tinged with pink. There are many cultivated varieties so that the fruit ranges widely in size, shape and flavor.

The CHINESE or SAND PEAR *Pyrus pyrifolia* is sparingly grown with us but has been crossed with *communis* to give the KIEFFER and other hybrid varieties.

The juice drink made from pears is known as perry.

Figure 111

83a Fruit retaining calyx lobes. Fig. 112......APPLE *Pyrus malus* L.

a, branch with flowers and young fruit; b, section of apple; c, section through a flower.

This is one of our best known fruits. It is represented by so many varieties that the trees and their fruit are quite variable. The trees are often low (sometimes 40 ft. or more), round topped, usually with oval pubescent leaves. The ripe fruit takes various shades of red, yellow, and green. The flowers are 1 to 2 inches across and tinged with pink.

Our present day choice varieties are mutants which have been selected from great numbers of seedlings. They are propagated and held true to type by budding or grafting. Trees raised from their seeds yield

Figure 112

"seeding" apples which are usually somewhat similar to the wild parent, though an occasional one might be highly superior.

83b Fruit when mature without calyx lobes; fruit yellow to red with waxy-like appearance. Fig. 113.................................
..............................SIBERIAN CRAB *Pyrus baccata* L.

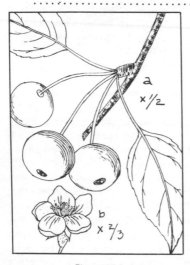

a, fruiting branch; b, flower.

This is a fairly large wide-topped tree originally from East Asia. Its flowers are white and smaller than those of the apple. The fruit is red and yellow with a translucent waxy-appearing flesh, and often small (only a fraction of an inch in diameter).

There are several Crabs that have a limited use for food. Some are native American species and others are hybrids of *baccata* and the apple or of some other crab.

The PRAIRIE CRAB *Pyrus ioensis* Bailey produces a profusion of pink flowers that beautify our Mid-Western woods in springtime, and hard green "apples" with a pleasing wild flavor. In our Eastern-states it gives place to the GARLAND CRAB *Pyrus coronaria* L. which closely resembles it.

Figure 113

SOULARDS CRAB has larger fruit. It is likely a hybrid.

84a Fruit a legume (pod opening at two opposite sides with the one-to-many seeds all attached at the same side. Usually with pea shaped flowers. Herbs, vines, shrubs or trees; leaves usually compound. Figs. 114-126...85

84b Not as in 84a...95

85a Herbaceous plants..86

85b An evergreen tree to 50 feet high. Flowers red. Fig. 114........
...................................CAROB *Ceratonia siliqua* **L.**

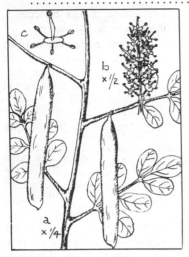

Figure 114

a, branch with fruit and leaves; b, inflorescence; c, single flower.

This tropical or near tropical evergreen tree bears a large amount of fruit used as food for man and his domestic animals. The flowers are small and bright red. The fruit a thickened pod up to 12 inches long has only a few small hard seeds, but is filled with a sweet pulp which contributes most of the food value. Other common names are St. Johns-Bread, Locust Bean, Honey Bread and Algaroba.

It seems that this was not the "locusts" eaten by Saint John, for that was the grasshoppers of his region, a then much used food, but the Carob could very likely have been the husks the prodigal son fed to the swine in his care.

86a Leaflets lateral and even numbered, the leaf often terminating in a tendril or bristle...87

86b Leaves with 3 leaflets one of which is terminal...............89

87a Pod ripening under ground, wrinkled, constricted between seeds; flowers yellow. Fig. 115..COMMON PEANUT *Arachis hypogaea* **L.**

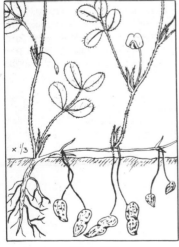

Figure 115

The Peanut is native of Brazil and is grown commercially in long season, mild-climated regions. It attains a height of 1 to 2 feet. The rather conspicuous yellow flowers are sterile, but less showy fertile flowers after pollination are pushed into the ground by their elongating pedicels where the nut matures. It is unusual for a fruit to thus develop under ground. The nuts contain from 1 to 4 seeds, and are roasted before being eaten or made into Peanut Butter, oil or Peanut Meal.

Other names are Ground Nut and Goober.

87b Pod ripening above ground................................88

88a (b,c) Seeds spherical, (sometimes flattened by close contact in pod), often wrinkled when dry; flowers ½ to ¾ inch, white; sepals leaf-like. Fig. 116...............GARDEN-PEA *Pisum sativum* L.

a, leaves and fruit; b, flower; c, tendril; d, stipule.

Peas, like most of the cultivated plants, are highly variable. Much greater differences than would be accounted necessary to make a new species with wild plants, can be given little attention in classifying cultigens to species. The plant has pinnated leaves with the terminal leaflet modified into a branched tendril (c); a pair of stipules (d) are often larger than the leaflets. The normal form is climbing and may reach a height of 6 feet; the flowers are white and the pods flattened. A low bush form (var. *humile*) is frequently raised in gardens.

Figure 116

It is ordinarily only the green or ripe seeds that are eaten but one strain has edible pods (var. *macrocarpon*).

The FIELD PEA, var. *arvense*, raised as forage, is characterized by pinkish flowers that have purple wings and a green keel.

88b Seeds flattened, circular; sepals long, slender, pointed; flowers, small, whitish. Fig. 117............LENTIL *Lens culinaris* Medic.

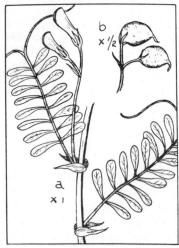

a, leaves and flowers; b, fruit.

This legume growing from 1 to 1½ feet high is much raised in Europe.' Two rounded seeds are borne in each pod. These are used when fully ripe, in soups and stews. The plants are fed to domestic animals. The flowers are whitish and less than ½ inch long. The seeds are yellowish brown and lens shaped, hence the name. It will be noted that many plants used for food bear the species name "esculenta."

Figure 117

88c Seeds large, flattened and angled; flowers 1 to 1½ in. long, white with purple markings, sepals short and broad. Fig. 118.........
............,..........................BROAD BEAN *Vicia faba* **L.**

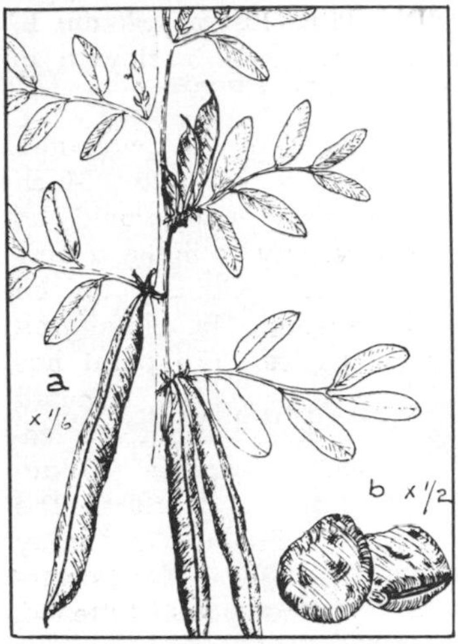

a, leaves and fruit; b, seeds.

This annual grows to a possible height of 6 feet. The flowers are more than an inch in length, whitish with a spot of purple. The fruit is long and heavy with the seed varying in size and shape but usually thick and often an inch across.

Broad Beans do not thrive well in our climate so have never become popular in America.

Other names are Windsor and Horse Bean.

Figure 118

89a Style bearded (hairy) near apical end.......................90

89b Stems and leaves with many brown hairs. Style smooth near apical end. Bushy field annual 2-6 feet, much raised as a farm crop. Fig. 119....................,.SOY-BEAN *Glycine max* **Merr.**

a, branch of plant; b, flower.

This plant has been introduced from China and Japan and has become a highly important farm crop, and a source of oil for food and other uses. The yield in the United States in 1956 totaled 455,869,000 bushels, which was a sharp increase over the ten year average of 271,-689,000 bushels.

It grows to a height of 2-6 feet, with small white or lavender flowers. There are many varieties and the globular seeds vary much in color and markings.

Soy-beans are frequently cut and threshed in the field by using a combine.

Figure 119

69

90a (b,c) Keel of corolla twisted spirally; leaves without tendrils. See Fig. 123b .... ,...92

90b Keel curved but not twisted into a coil; pods long and slender. See Fig. 122c 91

90c Keel bent inward at right angle, pods short and broad. Fig. 120.
.... **HYACINTH-BEAN** *Dolichos lablab* L.

This bean is grown both for food and as an ornamental. It is usually a climber and may reach a length of 20-30 feet. The flowers vary from white to deep purple and are nearly an inch across; the pods are 2-3 inches long, flattened and often purple. The seeds are white, purple or black.

Other names are Bonavist and Lablab.

It probably originated in the tropics where it is a perennial, but with us it is raised as an annual.

Figure 120

91a Slim hanging pods 1 to 2 feet long or longer. Fig. 121 ....
.... **ASPARAGUS-BEAN** *Vigna sesquipedalis* Wight

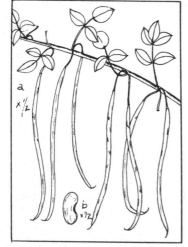

a, vine with pods; b, seed.

This, also known as the "Yard-Long Bean," is grown as a curiosity as well as for food. The pods are slender but sometimes actually reach a length of 3 feet or more. They are often much shriveled. The flowers are yellowish or violet, 2/3 to 1 inch long; the leaves attain a length of 5 inches. The seeds are about ½ inch long.

This bean likely originated in China and has long been cultivated in Europe.

Figure 121

91b Pods 6-12 inches long, hanging. Fig. 122......................
.............................COW-PEA *Vigna sinensis* Endl.
a, leaves and fruit; b, seeds; c, flower.

This plant's principal use is for forage and soil improvement, but the seeds are often used for food. It is a vigorous grower and produces pods 8-12 inches long with heavy seeds ¼-½ inch long of several colors and variable markings.

It seems to have originated in Asia.

The YAM-BEAN *Pachyrhizus tuberosus* Spr. is an important tropical food plant. Not only the young pods, but the tuberous roots are eaten. The terminal leaflets are lobed; the flowers are purplish and the pods up to 6 inches long.

Figure 122

92a Seeds flattened and broad, often about as wide as long........93

92b Seeds smaller, oblong or globular in shape. Calyx bracts as large or larger than the calyx. Fig. 123............................
..........................KIDNEY-BEAN *Phaseolus vulgaris* L.
a, plant with fruit; b, flower.

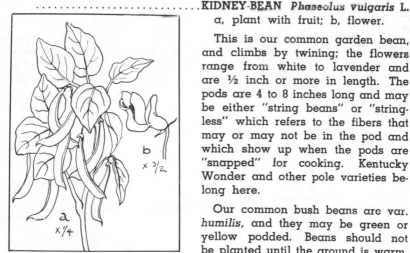

This is our common garden bean, and climbs by twining; the flowers range from white to lavender and are ½ inch or more in length. The pods are 4 to 8 inches long and may be either "string beans" or "stringless" which refers to the fibers that may or may not be in the pod and which show up when the pods are "snapped" for cooking. Kentucky Wonder and other pole varieties belong here.

Our common bush beans are var. *humilis*, and they may be green or yellow podded. Beans should not be planted until the ground is warm.

Figure 123

93a Flowers ½ inch or over, usually scarlet, though white in one variety. Fig. 124..........SCARLET RUNNER *Phaseolus coccineus* **L.**

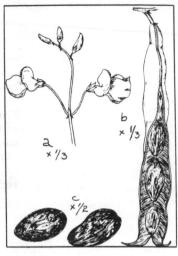

This one, known also as the Multiflora Bean is often raised as an ornamental. The flowers are bright scarlet and nearly an inch long. The pods are plump and 4 to 12 inches long, with seeds up to an inch in length, black or dark with red markings. It comes from tropical America.

Var. *albus* is the WHITE DUTCH RUNNER with while flowers and seeds.

Bush forms of both of the above are grown.

Figure 124

93b Flowers ⅛ to ⅜ inch long, whitish or cream colored..........94

94a Pods large with rolled edge; calyx bracts slim. Fig. 125..........
......................LIMA BEAN *Phaseolus limensis* **Macfad.**

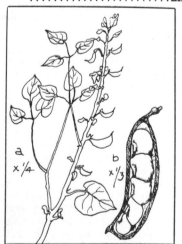

a, branch with flower and young fruit; b, pod with beans.

This tropical American bean is a perennial and in frost-free areas will continue to grow and produce for several years. In temperate regions it is raised as an annual. The pods are tough and woody so that only the shelled beans are eaten. These are marketed either green or dry. These seeds are often an inch broad and ¼ inch thick.

DWARF or BUSH LIMA is the variety *limenanus* which requires less care to raise.

Beans are high in protein and have long been included in man's list of foods.

Figure 125

94b Pods long beaked with sharp edges; calyx bracts broadly rounded with prominent veins. Fig. 126..SIEVA BEAN *Phaseolus lunatus* L.

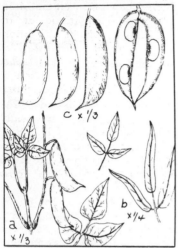

a, branch with fruit; b, types of leaves; c, types of pods.

This resembles the Lima Bean in shape of fruit and seeds. It too is likely of American origin. The leaflets are usually narrower than with the Limas. The greenish white flowers are small; the pods are 3-4 inches long by about an inch wide. The seeds are flat and thin and about ½ inch long. They are often white, but sometimes marked with red or brown in whole or part.

There are bush and narrow-leaved varieties.

Figure 126

95a Tropical glossy-leaved evergreen trees or shrubs; fruit globular or ovoid, of orange or lemon type. (hesperidium) See Figs. 127-134.
....**96**
95b Not as in 95a...**103**
96a Fruit with eight or more cells....................................**97**
96b Fruit with but 3 to 5 cells. Fig. 127..............................
..................**OVAL KUMQUAT** *Fortunella margarita* Swingle

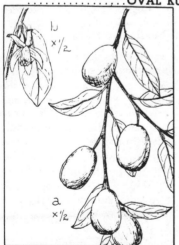

a, leaves and fruit; b, flower.

Kumquats are the dwarfs of the citrus group, these shrubs or small trees only reaching a height of 10 to 12 feet. The fruit of NAGAMI, here pictured, is oblong and only a little over an inch long with leaves 1½ to 3 inches in length. The flowers are fleshy, white and with 20 stamens, quite aromatic and are sometimes used for preserves or eaten raw.

Two other species, both with globular fruit are grown. MEIWA K. *Fortunella crassifolia* Sw. has an almost juiceless pulp while MARUMI K. *Fortunella japonica* Sw. has acid juice and is more prized for eating.

Figure 127

These plants are often raised as dwarf pot-plants. The fruit is eaten, —frequently, rind and all—and used in salads.

97a Petioles winged or margined, blades of leave attached to petiole in usual way..98

97b Leaves apparently un-attached to tip of petiole, petiole without wings; fruit with thick rind which is candied. Fig. 128.........
....CITRON *Citrus medica* L.

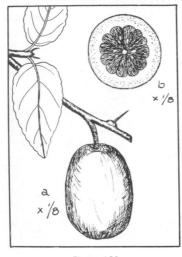

Figure 128

a, fruit and leaves; b, cross section of fruit.

The leaves of this shrub or tree grow from 4 to 8 inches long. The pale yellow, oblong, frequently roughened fruit reaches a length of 7 inches. The flowers are white with lilac exteriors and have about 30 stamens.

The pulp and juice is similar to the lemon but less acid. The spongy rind is the part most largely used. It is candied and used in fruit cakes, preserves, etc. It is grown, most largely, in the Mediterranean region, but also in Florida and California as a curiosity.

ETROG, used in Jewish ceremonies, is the wild form of the Citron.

98a Leaf petioles winged, flower buds white......................99

98b Leaf petioles margined but not winged; flower buds tinted with pink on outside; fruit very sour. Fig. 129...........................
..................................LEMON *Citrus limonia* Osbeck.

Figure 129

a, branch with flowers and fruit; b, cross section of a lemon.

California produces most of the lemons on our markets. It is a small thorny tree with leaves 2½ to 4 inches long. The flowers are white with pinkish exterior.

Lemons are picked green when they will no longer go through a ring 2¼ inches in diameter. They are put in cold storage and treated, to give them color as they are needed.

Several varieties are raised. In one the fruit may attain a length of almost 10 inches.

74

99a Flowers more than 1 inch across; fruit spherical or flattened at poles, mildly sour or sweet..................................**100**

99b Flowers less than 1 inch across, fruit elongated at poles, 1 to 2 inches in diameter, juice very sour. Fig. 130....................

..............................**LIME** *Citrus aurantifolia* Swingle

a, branch with leaves and thorns; b, cross section of fruit.

These thickly branched trees bear leaves 2-3 inches long. The flowers are white and about ½ inch across. The fruit is often much smaller than that of the lemon but limes much larger are common in southern Florida. The juice is highly acid. It is used in much the same way as the lemon.

The LIMEQUAT has been produced by crossing the Lime with the Oval Kumquat. It produces a pale yellow fruit a little less than 3 inches long.

Figure 130

100a Fruit less than 4 inches in diameter, deep yellow to vermillion when ripe; twigs glabrous..................................**101**

100b Fruit usually 4 inches or more in diameter, pale yellow; twigs pubescent. Fig. 131...........**GRAPEFRUIT** *Citrus paradisi* Sw.

a, branch with fruit; b, cross section of fruit.

Evidence points to the grapefruit having originated as a sport in the West Indies in the early part of the 19th century. It is a large, round-topped glossy-leaved tree which bears its fruit in axillary clusters from which it has derived its name.

The leaves are 3 to 6 inches long, with a characteristic broad-winged petiole. The white flowers are about one inch across, while the pale yellow fruit, often greenish or rust colored, has a diameter of 4 to 6 inches. The flesh is normally pale yellow, though there are pink fleshed varieties, and seedless forms.

Figure 131

The SHADDOCK or PUMMELO (*Citrus maxima* Merr.) is much like the Grapefruit. Its fruit is large, weighing as much as seven pounds each.

101a Leaf petioles with narrow wings.........................102

101b Leaf petioles with very broad wings; fruit acid. Fig. 132.......
....................SEVILLE ORANGE *Citrus aurantium* L.

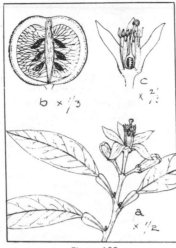

Figure 132

a, branch with leaves and flowers; b, longitudinal section through fruit; c, flower section.

This "Sour Orange" is grown in Southern Europe for use in beverages and preserves. Perfumery is made from the flowers. It is a medium-sized, much-spined tree with leaves some 4 inches in length, very fragrant white flowers, and globular fruit about 3 inches in diameter. This species is hardier than other citrus plants and is much used as stock on which other species are grafted.

The TRIFOLIATE ORANGE *Poncirus trifoliata* is a hardy ornamental with small orange-like fruit.

102a Outer covering of fruit tight; juice sweet. Fig. 133............
............................ORANGE, *Citris sinensis* Osbeck.

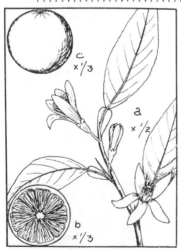

Figure 133

a, flowers and foliage; b, section through fruit; c, fruit.

This "Sweet Orange" seems to have originated in Southeast Asia. The trees are medium sized, with flowers white and very fragrant. It is now grown at many favorable places along our southern border from Florida to California.

It is desirable to supply the market throughout the entire twelve months. To do this, different varieties of oranges are raised. In California the Naval Orange from Brazil is on the market from November till April when the Valencias (from Spain) begin to ripen and are marketable until November.

Other orange raising regions cover the seasons with varieties suited to their growing conditions.

102b Fruit sweet; outer covering loose when ripe; segments usually exceeding 10. Fig. 134.. ....SATSUMA ORANGE ***Citrus nobilis* var. *unshiu*** **Swingle**

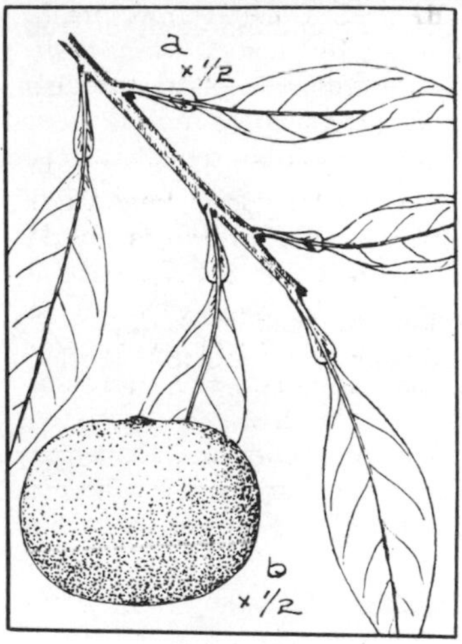

Figure 134

a, foliage; b, fruit.

Citrus nobilis is a thornless species with small white flowers and much flattened fruit with rough loose skin of a vermilion shade. Its juice is very sweet.

The Satsuma (var. *unshiu*) is a hardy variety with delightful flavor.

The TANGARINE and MANDARIN ORANGES (var. *delicosa*) have similar but smaller fruit than the Satsuma.

The CALAMONDIN *Citrus mitis* Blanco, bears sperical fruit 1 to 1½ in. in diameter. The color is a deep reddish orange. The juice is so sour that it substitutes nicely for limes or lemons.

103a Herbs with small flowers borne in umbels (a) (usually compound). Fruit dry, splitting into 2 seeds (b). Fig. 135....104

Figure 135

103b Plants not as in 103a.......................................115

104a (b,c) Fleshy underground parts used for food..............105

104b Leaves eaten 107

104c Fruit ("seeds") used for seasoning........................109

105a Fleshy tap root eaten.....................................106

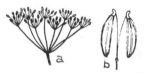

105b Tuberous roots eaten. Leaves once-pinnately compound, flowers white. Fig. 136.......................SKIRRET *Sium sisarum* L.

a, branch with leaves and fruit; b, pinnately compound leaf; c, fruit.

This Eastern Asiatic plant has been used in Europe for its edible roots much as the vegetable oyster is used. The roots have a woody core which needs to be removed and which detracts from its popularity.

The plant reaches a height of 2-3 feet. The leaves have 3 to 7 leaflets. The flowers are white.

The clustered tuber-like roots may be left in the ground over winter or dug in the fall and stored for winter use.

Figure 136

106a (b,c) Roots yellow to deep orange, flowers white, leaves finely cut. Fig. 137..
........CULTIVATED CARROT *Daucus carota* var. *sativa* (DC.)

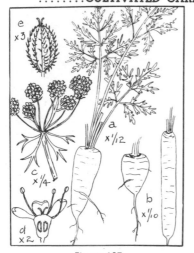

a, plant with edible root; b, other forms of roots; c, compound umbel with flowers; d, flower section; e, fruit.

Don't neglect your carrots if your eyes need help. This once lowly, and not too well liked vegetable has been boosted into a "must" from the health viewpoint. Its raising and marketing has become a large industry.

Var. *sativa* is usually a biennial and has a thick tap-root that runs to several shapes with the different varieties. The deep yellow to salmon-red color is evidence of the carotin it contains. Var. *carota* is the wild or escaped carrot sometimes known as Queen Anne's Lace, the name

Figure 137

referring to its flat topped finely divided inflorescence of tiny white flowers. Its root is slim and rather woody.

The plant attains a height of 3 feet when in bloom. This is usually the spring of the second year, although it sometimes behaves as an annual.

106b Roots tapering, white; flowers greenish-yellow, leaves pinnately compound, with coarse leaflets. Fig. 138......................
....................CULTIVATED PARSNIP *Pastinaca sativa* L.

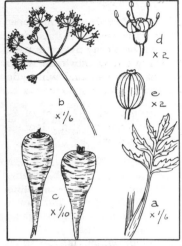

Figure 138

a, leaf; b, compound umbel of flowers; c, typical roots; d, single flower; e, fruit.

Like the Carrot, the Parsnip has both a wild and cultivated variety. The escape form with slender inedible root is widely naturalized in waste land. It is var. *sylvestris*.

This perennial reaches a height of 5 feet the second year when it produces its greenish-yellow flowers and seeds. The grooved stems are coarse and hollow. The fleshy tap roots may live out of doors through the winter and seem to be the better for being frozen. The root flesh is a dull white.

Parsnips have been cultivated since the days of early Rome.

106c Root globular with several thick branches below, white inside; flowers white; leaves pinnately compound. Fig. 139..........
...............CELERIAC *Apium graveolens* var. *rapaceum* DC.

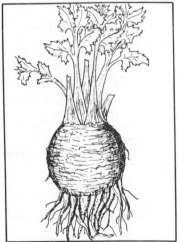

Figure 139

This is only a less known form of the common Celery. In this case the reserve plant food has been stored in a thick turnip-like root which has about the same flavor as celery.

It has greater favor in Europe than with us. It is used for flavoring, cooked in soups and stews, put into salads or eaten by itself. Other names are Knob Celery, German Celery and Turnip Celery.

107a Entire leaf used for seasoning or garnishing...............108

107b Thickened petiole eaten raw or cooked. Fig. 140..............
.....................CELERY *Apium graveolens* var. *dulce* DC.

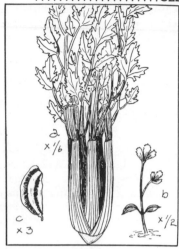

Figure 140

a, typical bunch of celery; b, seedling; c, celery seed.

There is a short thick stem (heart) which supports the roots below and from which the fleshy-petioled leaves arise. The plant is marketed at the end of the first season. During the second year flowers and seeds are produced. The flowers are white and borne in compounds umbels. Celery seed is ground to make celery salt or used ground or whole in pickles and relishes.

Various schemes of "blanching" the stalks are used, such as putting boards on each side of the row or banking with earth. In more recent years it is marketed green. The threads so apparent in the stalks (leaf petioles) are the vascular bundles of the transporting system.

108a (b,c) Leaflets divided into 3 parts, flowers greenish-yellow. Fig.
141.....................PARSLEY *Petroselinum crispum* Mansf.

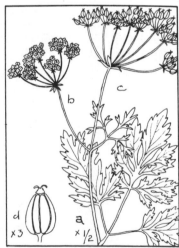

Figure 141

a, branch with leaf; inflorescence of flowers (b), and of seeds (c); d, fruit.

The leaves of this low-growing plant are used for garnishing and for seasoning. It seems to have originally come from Egypt but has been much raised in Europe and America. The flowering and fruiting stalks may attain a height of 2 feet. The flowers are greenish.

The common parsley often has leaves as here pictured but a variety with much curled leaves is a strong favorite.

TURNIP-ROOTED or HAMBURG PARSLEY var. *radicosum* has thick white roots 2 inches by 6 or 8 inches long, resembling parsnips and is used in much the same way.

108b Leaflets not in 3's, finely cut; flowers white. Fig. 142............
................SALAD CHERVIL *Anthriscus cerefolium* Hoffm.

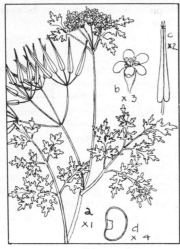

Figure 142

a, branch with leaf and fruit; b, flower; c, fruit; d, cross section of seed.

This is a some-what hairy annual that grows to a height of about 2 feet. The flowers are white and the fruit elongated and black. The leaves resemble parsley. It is used in salads and soups. There is a curled leaf variety.

TURNIP-ROOTED CHERVIL, *Chaerophyllum bulbosum* L. is raised for its 2-4 inch long underground tubers, which are carrot-like but grayish or blackish.

108c. Leaflets not in 3's finely cut; flowers yellow. DILL.........111a

109a Fruit not bristly; plants 1 to 3 ft. high or higher..............110

109b Fruit bristly; plants only about 6 inches high; flowers white or rose. Fig. 143....................CUMIN *Cuminum cyminum* L.

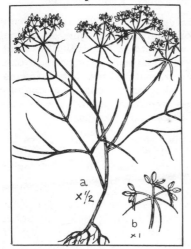

Figure 143

a, entire plant; b, branch of fruiting head.

This little annual herb gets up to only six inches. The leaves are finely cut and the flowers white or rose-tinted. The small seeds are used for spicing or flavoring many food products such as soups, salads, bread, cheese and pickles.

It has been long known in Europe and Asia. Several herbs of this family are mentioned in the Bible, this being one of them.

110a Fruit nearly spherical; outer flowers of each secondary umbel with petals ray like. Fig. 144.....................................
...........................CORIANDER *Coriandrum sativum* **L.**

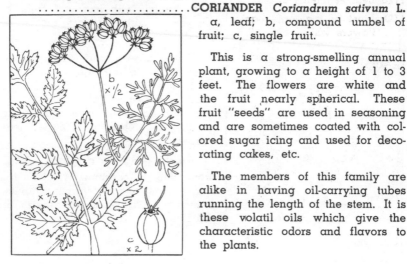

a, leaf; b, compound umbel of fruit; c, single fruit.

This is a strong-smelling annual plant, growing to a height of 1 to 3 feet. The flowers are white and the fruit nearly spherical. These fruit "seeds" are used in seasoning and are sometimes coated with colored sugar icing and used for decorating cakes, etc.

The members of this family are alike in having oil-carrying tubes running the length of the stem. It is these volatil oils which give the characteristic odors and flavors to the plants.

Figure 144

111a Leaves very finely cut so that ultimate divisions are linear; fruit flattened. Fig. 145.................DILL *Anethum graveolens* **L.**

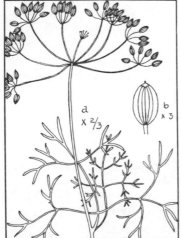

a, branch with leaves and compound umbel of fruit; b, fruit.

This plant is best known through its contribution to the pickles which bears its name. It reaches a height of 2 to 3 feet with smooth stems and finely-divided leaves. The flowers are yellowish green. The slightly winged seeds are employed in flavoring sauces and pickles.

Some prefer to use the leaves instead of the seeds as they have seemingly a better flavor. The plant is of European origin.

Figure 145

111b Outer segments of leaves broader; fruit not flattened.......112

112a Leaf segments in 3's.....................................113

112b Most of the leaf segments not in 3's; fruit elongated, curved; flowers white. Fig. 146.............CARAWAY *Carum carvi* L.

a, leaves, flowers, fruit; b, flower in detail; c, single fruit.

This biennial plant is usually about 2 feet high. The flowers are white and the seeds elongated.

The seeds are put into bread and cheese, as well as being used for candy and perfume making. The plant has a fleshy tap root not unlike the parsnip. This root is eaten as a vegetable. The roots and young shoots are sometimes used in stews.

The plant is a native of Germany and Holland but sometimes grows spontaneously with us.

Figure 146

113a Leaf petioles thickened; flowers white. Seed ground into "celery salt." Fig. 140. CELERY.................................107b

113b Flowers yellowish; petioles not thickened...................114

114a Flowers greenish-yellow; stems heavy. Fig. 147...............
.........................LOVAGE *Levisticum officinale* Koch.

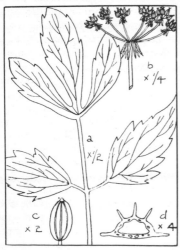

a, leaf; b, inflorescence of fruit; c, fruit; d, cross section of seed.

Lovage is a native of Italy. The stems, leaves, and tender shoots are sometimes used in salad and stews but it is the seed which is principally employed for food as in candy making or other seasoning.

The plant is a perennial; it may attain a height of 6 feet and has coarsely-toothed, three-parted leaves. The flowers are greenish-yellow or sometimes pinkish. Other names are Italian Lovage and Garden Lovage.

Figure 147

114b Flowers yellowish-white, annual. Fig. 148.....................
.................................ANISE *Pimpinella anisum* **L.**

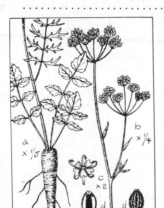

Figure 148

a, root and leaves; b, fruiting branch with flowers and seeds; c, flower in detail; d, side and edge views of fruit (2 seeds).

The plant has a height of about 2 feet. The flowers are yellowish-white and small. It belongs to the Mediterranean countries and Germany. The seeds and oil are used in candy and cookie making.

The German anise cakes are an essential part of the Christmas season in many homes.

115a Petals united into a tubular corolla, usually with two lips (a); plant stems usually square in cross section (b); plants characterized by their volatile oil. Fig. 149. MINT FAMILY 116

Figure 149

115b Plants not as in 115a.....................................122
116a Flowers with four perfect stamens...........................117
116b With but two perfect stamens; leaves and stems white, woolly. Flowers blue, purple or white. Fig. 150........................
....................................SAGE *Salvia officinalis* **L.**

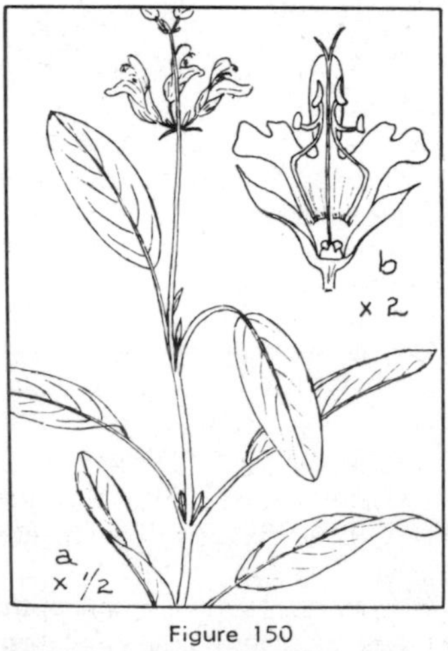

a, branch with leaves and flowers; b, section of flower showing parts.

This semi-shrubby perennial, 6 to 15 inches high, is grown in many gardens, for its leaves and stems make a favorite seasoning for sausages, dressings, etc. The leaves are usually gray with a whitish woolly growth. The flowers range from white to violet or blue. It is a native of the Mediterranean region.

It is used either fresh or dried.

SCARLET SAGE or "SALVIA" *Salvia splendens,* Ker. a Brazilian shrub growing to a height of 8 feet, is a very popular ornamental with us, where it is seen in yards and parks covered with a profusion of scarlet

Figure 150

flowers. The first frost kills it, so it is grown here as an annual.

Salvia is a very large genus with some 500 species known to science; many of them are shrubs. They are widely scattered geographically:

117a Floral bracts (leaves at base of flowers and fruit) about as large as the stem leaves..118

117b Floral bracts much smaller than the stem leaves..............119

118a Stamens longer than the corolla; leaves about 1/3 as wide as long. Fig. 151..................HYSSOP *Hyssopus officinalis* L.

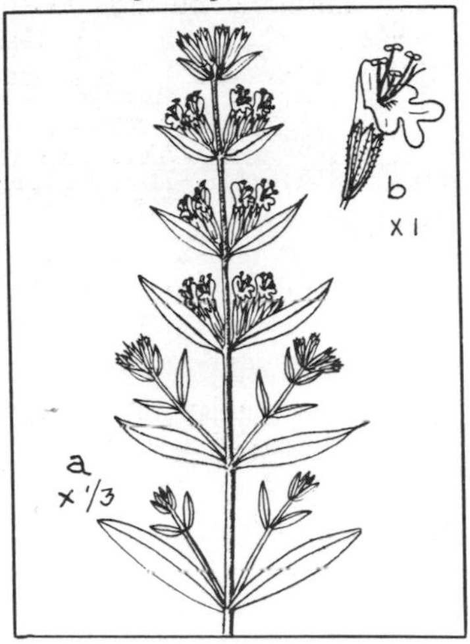

Figure 151

a, branch with flowers and leaves; b, leaves.

This little herb, growing about 15 to 20 inches high, finds use as a potherb and for flavoring. The leaves and young stems are used in salads and the flowers employed to flavor soup. "Hyssop tea" is made from the dried flowering branches. For this purpose they are picked while still in the bud stage.

The flowers are normally blue although var. *alba* has white flowers and in var. *ruber* the flowers are red.

118b Stamens about the same length as the corolla; leaves linear, about 1/6 as wide as long. Fig. 152..................................
.......................SUMMER SAVORY *Satureja hortensis* L.

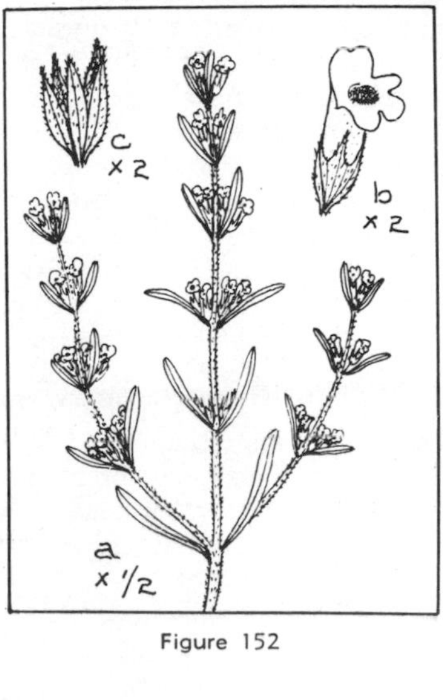

Figure 152

a, branch with flowers; b, flower; c, fruit.

This annual herb averages about a foot in height, with soft hairy leaves. The flowers vary from white to bluish to pink. It is a rather common escape having been introduced from Europe.

The leaves are used fresh, or dried for flavoring soups and dressings much the same as Sage.

WINTER SAVORY *Satureja montana* L. also known as Mountain Savory is a perennial which is similarly used.

Several other species of this genus, though less common, find occasional use for seasoning.

119a Leaves more than ½ inch wide.............................120

119b Leaves less than ¼ inch wide; plant less than 1 ft. high; flowers in open terminal clusters; calyx 2 lipped. Fig. 153.............

....THYME *Thymus vulgaris* L.

a, branch of plant; b, flower.

This little subshrub attains a height of only 6 or 8 inches and is covered with a whitish pubescence. The flowers are lilac colored. It is used for seasoning much like sage. For drying, the upper branches are picked when blossoming begins.

MOTHER-OF-THYME *Thymus serphyllum* L. has similar uses. It is prostrate in habit and is also called Creeping Thyme. Several varieties have been developed differing in the colors of flowers and leaves.

Both of these plants are natives of Southern Europe.

Figure 153

120a Teeth on leaves sharp pointed.............................121

120b Teeth on leaves rounded at tips. Fig. 154....................

....CATNIP *Nepeta cataria* L.

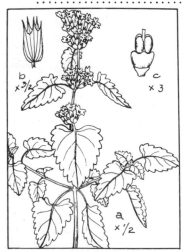

a, flowering branch; b, fruit; c, four-parted ovary characteristic of the mints.

This old-world plant is now widely scattered in America. It attains a height of some 3 feet, is soft with short pubescence and has pale lavender or pinkish flowers.

It is sometimes used for seasoning and for making "catnip tea." Its quality is best when first blooming. Cats are particularly fond of it. Other names are Catmint and Catnep.

Several other species of the genus are cultivated, mostly as bedding plants. GROUND IVY *Glechoma hederacea* L. is very common. It is a creeping plant with round or kidney-shaped leaves and bright blue flowers. It possesses a rather unpleasant odor.

Figure 154

121a Leaves sessile; spikes slim, scattered. Fig. 155..............
...............................SPEARMINT *Mentha spicata* **L.**

a, branch with leaves and flowers; b, single flower.

This glabrous, herbaceous perennial grows to a height of a foot or more and is a bright green with clear white flowers. It is a native of Europe but is widely naturalized in our country. Its chief use is in chewing gum though it also finds use as seasoning and for making a beverage.

APPLE MINT *Mentha rotundifolia* Huds. growing to a height of 30 inches with oval, pubescent leaves and purple flowers is highly regarded by some for seasoning.

Figure 155

121b Leaves with short petioles; spikes thick and compact. Fig. 156...
............................,........PEPPERMINT *Mentha piperita* **L.**

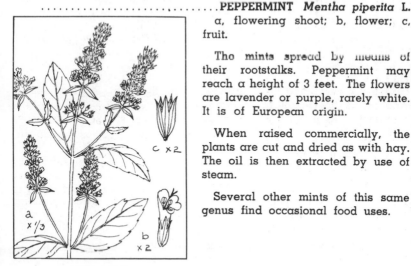

a, flowering shoot; b, flower; c, fruit.

The mints spread by means of their rootstalks. Peppermint may reach a height of 3 feet. The flowers are lavender or purple, rarely white. It is of European origin.

When raised commercially, the plants are cut and dried as with hay. The oil is then extracted by use of steam.

Several other mints of this same genus find occasional food uses.

Figure 156

122a Herbs (rarely shrubs) with star-shaped flowers and 2-5 celled, many seeded, fleshy berry (sometimes a dry capsule). Figs. 157-167. NIGHTSHADE FAMILY...............................123

123a Common succulent garden or field plant, bearing underground starchy tubers. Fig. 157........POTATO *Solanum tuberosum* L.

a, plant with tubers; b, flower; c, fruit (seed balls); d, longitudinal section of fruit showing seeds.

This highly important food plant is a native of South America. The plant is grown by planting pieces of the tubers raised the preceding year. The pieces must have at least one eye. The plant reaches a height of 1 to 3 feet and some varieties produce abundant white or lavender flowers and fruit balls. The fruit resembles small green tomatoes. The seed thus produced may be planted. The first year their tubers are small, but these small tubers will grow plants that produce normal sized potatoes. New varieties are secured this way, but these seedlings are often inferior to their parents. The yield in 1956 for our country was 2,437,180,000 pounds.

Figure 157

Tomato scions have been grafted on potato plants so that while potato tubers are produced underground, tomato fruit ripens on the same plant. This makes an interesting novelty, but has scant practical value.

124b Fruit dry with very fine seeds; leaves long and broad, used for smoking, chewing and snuff. Fig. 158........................
.............,.....................TOBACCO *Nicotiana tabacum* L.

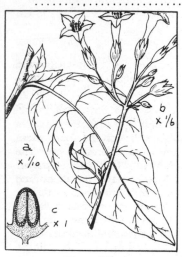

a, typical leaf; b, flowers; c, fruit showing seeds.

This annual plant growing to a height of several feet and producing long, broad leaves is a native of South America. The flowers are from 1½ to 2 inches long and pale pink to rose. The fruit is a dry capsule which contains many very small seeds. There are numerous varieties raised commercially.

Figure 158

125a Fruit not enveloped within an enlarged calyx...............126
125b Fruit greenish, yellow or purple berry, enclosed in a much enlarged sac-like calyx.......................................131
126a Fruit bluish-black or purplish when ripe.....................127
126b Fruit red or yellow when ripe............................128
127a Fruit ½ inch or less in diameter; flowers small, white with yellow center, plants glabrous. Fig. 159........................
..........................WONDERBERRY *Solanum nigrum* L.

a, branch with leaves and fruit; b, berry; c, flower.

This rather common weed has been changed by selection until the bluish-black berries grow to nearly ½ inch in diameter and are eaten raw or made into preserves, etc. The plant may reach a height of 3 feet. It has white flowers and is an abundant producer, but reverts to its smaller size if permitted to grow as a weed.

Other names are Garden Huckleberry, Morelle and Sunberry (var. *guineense*).

Figure 159

127b Fruit up to several inches in diameter; leaves large, irregular; gray, tomentose. Fig. 160.....................................
..................COMMON EGGPLANT *Solanum melongena* **L.**

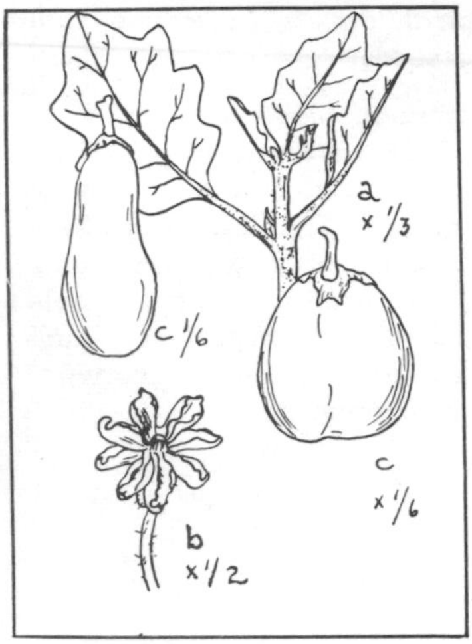

a, branch with leaves; b, flower; c, fruit.

This sturdy growing plant is usually covered with a long gray pubescence. The flowers are violet and nearly 2 inches across. The fruit is a large, smooth-skinned, rather solid-meated berry. The fruit varies much in shape, color and size. Purple is the common color though there are white, yellow and striped ones.

The SNAKE EGGPLANT var. *serpentinum* grows a fruit some 12 inches long but only an inch thick and curled. There is a dwarf variety producing flowers and fruit smaller than that of the Common Eggplant.

The SCARLET EGGPLANT *Solanum integrifolium* Poir. with scarlet or yellow fruit 2 inches across, is used as an ornamental.

Figure 160

128a Anthers closely surrounding the style. Fruit smooth.........129
128b Stamens and anthers spreading; fruit wrinkled or somewhat irregular 130
129a Tropical, tree-like, soft, hairy, woody shrub to 10 feet high. Leaves simple, cordate to a foot long. Fruit egg shaped, 3 inches long, dark red. Fig. 161....TREE-TOMATO *Cyphomandra betacea* **Sen.**

a, leaf; b, fruit.

This somewhat woody shrub grows to a height of 6 to 10 feet. The fragrant flowers are ½ inch across and pink. The egg shaped fruit is about 3 inches long. It is dark red or brownish and resembles the common tomato in flavor.

It is a tropical plant and can be grown only in greenhouses in temperate regions.

Figure 161

90

129b Leaves pinnately compound hairy, strong smelling; flowers yellow. Fig. 162...........TOMATO *Lycopersicon esculentum* Mill.

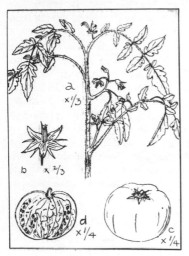

Figure 162

a, branch with leaves and flowers; b, flower; c, typical fruit; d, longitudinal section through fruit.

The young plants stand erect but topple over as they grow larger and begin to develop fruit. The vine may become 6 feet or more in length. The flowers are yellow, and the fruit yellow, scarlet or "purple" red.

Not so many years ago tomatoes were thought to be poisonous and were grown only for ornament and called "Loveapples." Their importance as a food has increased rapidly largely on account of their favorable vitamin contents.

Other botanical varieties are Cherry Tomato producing clusters of ¾ inch globular fruit, Pear Tomato about 1½ inch long and pear-shaped, Potato-Leaved Tomato and the Upright of Tree Tomato.

130a Fruit large puffy, depressed at base, variously shaped; mild flavor. Yellow or red when ripe. Fig. 163...............................
SWEET or BELL PEPPERS *Capsicum frutescens* var. *grossum* Bailey

Figure 163

a, branch with leaves and fruit; b, flower (5 petals are normal but cultigens often have extras); c, cross section of fruit showing many seeds.

This plant is really a tropical shrub but is grown with us as an annual, since the early frosts kill it. In frost-free areas it may reach a height of 8 feet, but in our one season, 2 to 3 feet is a good height. The leaves are glabrous and 1 to 5 inches long; the flowers are white or greenish-white. Fruit colors when ripe are yellow, red and dark violet. The Sweet Pepper is mild flavored and used in salads and relishes or "stuffed" and pickled.

**130b Fruit smaller than 130a, of various shapes; flavor usually fiery.
Fig. 164...................RED PEPPERS *Capsicum frutescens* L.**

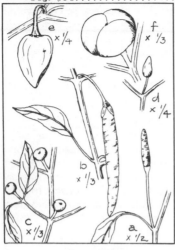

Figure 164

Under this heading it is chosen to include several groups of the species other than the Sweet Peppers. In this we follow Erwin.

TABASCO GROUP (a); erect, elongate, very "hot" fruit with cup-like calyx; flowers small. CAYENNE GROUP (b); called chili or finger peppers have long curved pods 4 to 12 inches in length. The calyx is cup-shaped. CHERRY GROUP (c); small globular fruit on long erect pedicels, orange or red. This and the groups that follow have saucer-shaped calyx cups. CELESTIAL GROUP (d); fruit ¾ to 1¼ inches long, erect first yellow-green then light purple and finally orange red. PERFECTION GROUP (e); pods 3 to 4 inches long, hanging, bright red. TOMATO GROUP (f); fruit 2-4 inches in diameter, usually with 4 cells, yellow or red. These are sometimes called Pimentos.

131a Stems pubescent or hairy; berry yellow when ripe...........132

**131b Stems glabrous; berry· purplish. Fig. 165.......................
..........................TOMATILLO *Physalis ixocarpa* Brot.**

Figure 165

a, branch with fruit in husks; b, flower; c, section through husk showing berry.

This glabrous annual grows to a height of 3 to 4 feet. The bright yellow flowers are ¾ inch across and have 5 brown spots in the throat. The inflated calyx as it surrounds the berry is purple veined. The berry is sticky, purple and many seeded. It has been introduced from Mexico.

If ground cherries when picked are left in the husk they will usually keep through the winter.

**132a Plants to 1 foot high, often prostrate, anthers yellow. Berry sticky when ripe. Fig. 166...
................STRAWBERRY-TOMATO** *Physalis pubescens* **L.**

Figure 166

a, branch with flowers and fruit; b, fruit in calyx and husk.

This plant usually grows prostrate and reaches a stem length of about a foot. The leaves are soft, and both they and the stems are pubescent. The flowers are less than ½ inch long and pale yellow with 5 brown spots in the throat. The anthers are yellow.

The calyx, rather short at flowering times, elongates to completely enclose the yellow fruit which becomes about ¾ inch in diameter.

This is the most common garden ground-cherry. The berries are eaten raw or cooked in several ways.

132b Plants to 3 feet high, anthers blue or purple; fruit not sticky when ripe. Fig. 167........CAPE-GOOSEBERRY *Physalis peruviana* **L.**

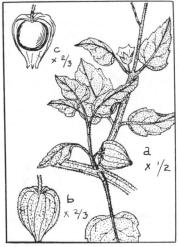

Figure 167

a, branch with flower and fruit; b, fruit in husk; c, husk split to show berry.

This species also bears a globular yellow berry which is not sticky. The plant is larger than the Strawberry-Tomato and more thickly covered with pubescence. Its berry is less sweet.

It may stand up to 3 feet high. The flowers are pale yellow and usually more than ½ inch across. There are purple spots and veins in the petals and the anthers are bluish-purple.

There are several wild members of this genus any of which could be eaten much the same as the three described here.

The **CHINESE LANTERN PLANT** *P. alkekengi* L. is very showy with large bright red calyx "pods."

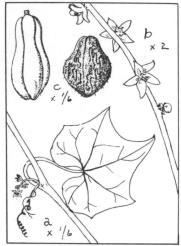

a, section of vine showing leaf, tendril and staminate flowers; b, staminate flowers; c, fruit.

This large tender vine grows from perennial tubers. The flowers are small and whitish. The fruit is usually pale green, 3 to 8 inches long and resembles a squash. It has but one seed, a flattened disk-like structure 1 to 2 inches across. The fruit, of which there may be 100 borne on one vine are used much the same as summer squashes.

The entire fruit is planted or new plants are raised from cuttings. It is popular in our southern-most states, where the underground parts live

Figure 168

year after year. In the tropics the large tubers are also eaten.

Other names are Mango Squash, Merliton and Christophine.

136a (b,c) Leaves prickly, deeply cut between the lobes; fruit stalk angular, expanding at point of attachment. Fig. 169............
..............FIELD AND OTHER PUMPKINS *Cucurbita pepo* L.

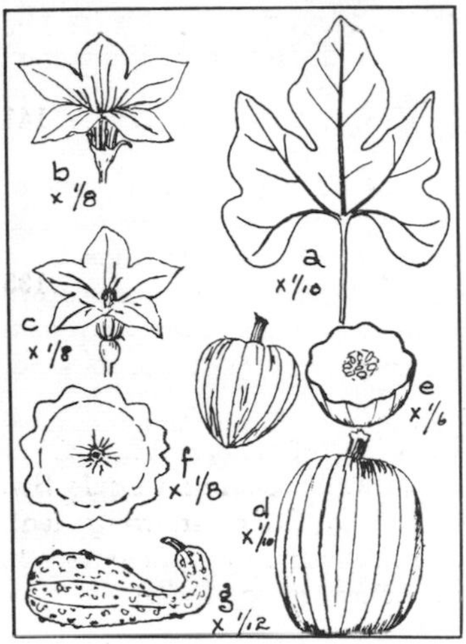

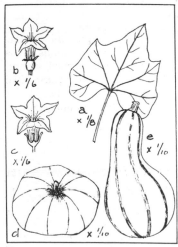

a, leaf; b, staminate flower; c, pistillate flower; d, field pumpkin; e, acorn "squash"; f, summer scallop "squash"; g, s u m m e r crookneck "squash."

Popular ideas are due for a startling awakening, when one studies this group. Some of the "squashes" he has been eating proved to be pumpkins and the great fruit taking the prize at the pumpkin show will most likely be a real squash.

This species was raised by the Indians before the coming of Columbus and is the one frequently used for pumpkin-pies.

Several of our so-called squashes also fall here as shown in the illustration.

Figure 169

The YELLOW-FLOWERED GOURDS var. *ovifera* with small deeply lobed leaves, and hard shelled fruit of many shapes and colors are raised for ornament or curiosity.

136b Leaves not feeling harsh or prickly; lobes pointed with but shallow cut between lobes; fruit stalk hard, angled and expanding at point of attachment. Fig. 170......................CHEESE, CUSHAW AND OTHER PUMPKINS *Cucurbita moschata* Duch.

a, leaf; b, pistillate flower; c, staminate flower; d, Pie Pumpkin; e, Cushaw.

The plants of this species feel soft as compared to the harsh prickly plants of *pepo*. The Cushaws and Winter Crooknecks bear abundantly and their large solid fruit may be used in several ways much as with the preceding species.

Pumpkins are often canned or dried and are sometimes made into pumpkin meal. They were frequently raised in corn fields with out seeming to seriously reduce the corn yield, but the coming of husking machines has put a stop to that practice.

Figure 170

136c Leaves not feeling harsh or prickly; lobes rounded with shallow cuts between; fruit stalk thick and soft, spongy, round in cross section. Fig. 171..........SQUASHES *Cucurbita maxima* Duch.

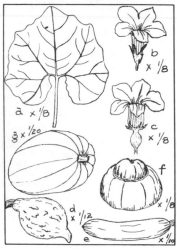

a, leaf; b, staminate flower; c, pistillate flower; d, Hubbard Squash; e, Banana Squash; f, Turban (Buttercup) Squash; g, Mammoth Squash.

The thickened, somewhat soft stem is one of the best characters for distinguishing these true squashes from the pumpkins. The flesh is usually an orange-yellow and firm. Squashes are particularly good for baking.

The Mammoth Chile Squash may attain a weight of 200 pounds or more and be larger than a washtub. It must have been one of this species which "Peter, Peter, Pumpkin Eater" used for clothing his wife.

Figure 171

137a Sepals small, with smooth margins, not turning black towards base **138**

**137b Sepals comparatively large, leaf-like, reflexed, their margins notched. Fig. 172...
.......CHINESE PRESERVING MELON** *Benincasa hispida* Cogn.

This annual vine produces long (up to 16 inches) waxy-white fruit which is covered with hairs. The thick flesh is white and is chiefly used in preserves, although it is sometimes eaten raw. The flowers are yellow and 3 inches across. The seeds are about ½ inch long.

Other names are Zit-Kwa Tunka, Wax Gourd and Chinese Watermelon.

Figure 172

138a Tendrils not branched; leaves not pinnately lobed...........139

138b Tendrils branched; leaves pinnately lobed. Fig. 173...........
......................WATERMELON *Citrullus vulgaris* **Schrad.**

Figure 173

a, vine with staminate flowers; b, pistillate flower; c, fruit; d, cross section of fruit.

The watermelon is a native of Africa and is our most popular fruit of its types. The vines seem rather fragile but run to some distance and bear profusely, often 12 tons or more per acre. There are many varieties as seen by their shapes, colors and markings. The flesh is usually red, though there are yellow fleshed varieties. The seeds may be either black or white. The flowers are yellow.

The CITRON, a hard white fleshed variety (var. *citroides*) is used for making preserves.

139a Fruit spiny or roughened with hard points used green for pickeling 140

139b Fruit smooth or covered with slightly raised net design, not spiny.
Fig. 174....................,..........MUSKMELON *Cucumis melo* **L.**

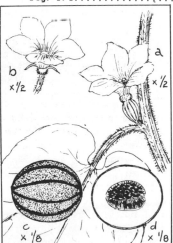

Figure 174

a, leaf and pistillate flower; b, staminate flower; c, fruit; d, longitudinal section of fruit.

This soft hairy vine with angled stems, bears leaves 3 to 5 inches and yellow flowers about an inch across. It runs to many varieties,— NUTMEG MELONS var. *reticulatus* has small fruit with netted surface; CANTALOUPE MELONS var. *cantalupensis* with hard rinds often furrowed or rough; WINTER MELON var. *inodorus*, flowers and fruit large; keeping through winter; SNAKE MELON var. *flexuosus*, fruit 18-40 inches long and 1-3 inches thick; MANGO MELON var. *chito*, fruit 2 to 3 inches through, flesh white, used for preserves and pickles.

140a Leaves deeply lobed with enlarged rounded sinuses; fruit heavily prickeled and 2 inches or less long with many seeds. Fig. 175....
............................**BUR GHERKIN** *Cucumis anguria* L.

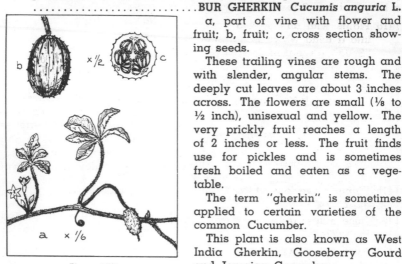

a, part of vine with flower and fruit; b, fruit; c, cross section showing seeds.

These trailing vines are rough and with slender, angular stems. The deeply cut leaves are about 3 inches across. The flowers are small (⅛ to ½ inch), unisexual and yellow. The very prickly fruit reaches a length of 2 inches or less. The fruit finds use for pickles and is sometimes fresh boiled and eaten as a vegetable.

The term "gherkin" is sometimes applied to certain varieties of the common Cucumber.

This plant is also known as West India Gherkin, Gooseberry Gourd and Jamaica Cucumber.

Figure 175

140b Leaves scarcely lobed, with sharp sinuses, if at all. Fruit larger. Fig. 176.......................CUCUMBER *Cucumis sativus* L.

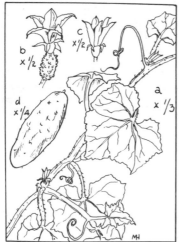

a, vine with leaves; b, pistillate flower with inferior ovary (young fruit); c, staminate flower; d, a cucumber.

The fruit of this plant furnishes the material for most of the pickles used in our country. The vine is harsh and prickly and is supplied with tendrils for climbing, but is usually grown in open fields where it trails over the ground. The bright yellow flowers measure about 1½ inches across. The fruit is usually picked while young and small. More nearly mature cucumbers are used for slicing and in salads.

When ripe the fruit is orange yellow and of but little use for food.

Dill pickles are made by natural fermentation of the cucumbers in water or brine much the same as sauerkraut. Dill and other spices are added for their flavor.

Figure 176

The ENGLISH FORCING CUCUMBER var. *angilicus* is a coarser plant with large leaves and flowers. The fruit is slender but may attain a length of 2 to 3 feet and without spines.

141a Plants with one or two kinds of usually small flowers crowded into a head which is surrounded by a ring (involucre) of bracts. "Seed" an achene. Fig. 177. COMPOSITAE 142

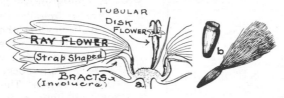

Fig. 177. .a, diagram of cross section of composite flower ;b, achenes.

141b Plants of various structures and many uses but apparently not as in 141a 147

142a Juice milky; all flowers in the head ligulate (strap-shaped). See Fig. 177a 143

142b Juice not milky; both tubular and ligulate flowers in the head. See Fig. 177a 146

143a Flowers blue or lavender 144

143b Flowers yellow. Fig. 178 .... **LETTUCE** *Lactuca sativa* L.

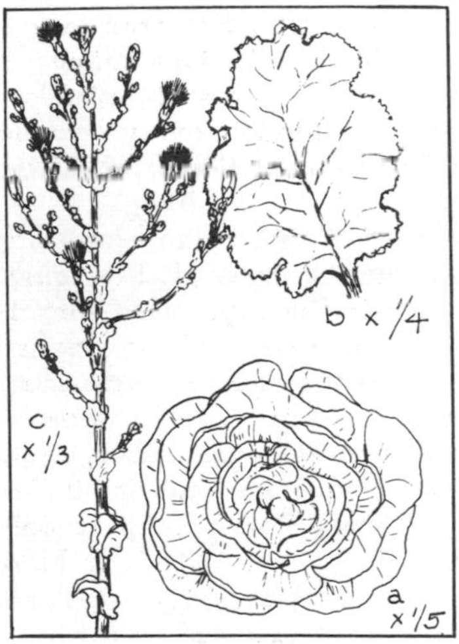

a, plant of head lettuce; b, leaf of leaf lettuce; c, top of fruiting stalk with flowers and seeds.

Lettuce has been much used for many years but the more recent interest in green vegetables, vitamins, etc., has greatly increased the demand for it. This annual first grows a rosette of many crisp leaves then presently a flowering stem arises to a height of 2-4 feet. Many tiny flowers with yellow rays appear in each composite head, followed, of course, by the seeds.

CURLED LETTUCE var. *crispa* is the home garden type, producing "leaf lettuce."

HEAD LETTUCE var. *capita* is sold in abundance at the markets.

Figure 178

COS and ROMAINE LETTUCE var. *longifolia* grow in erect-column heads.

ASPARAGUS LETTUCE var. *angustana*, least generally known, is grown for its thick edible stems.

144a Leaves lobed and cut, often much convoluted: flowering heads sessile 145

144b Long tapering straight leaves with uncut margins; seed plume attached to seed by a peduncle. Fig. 179 .... SALSIFY *Tragopogon porrifolius* L.

Figure 179

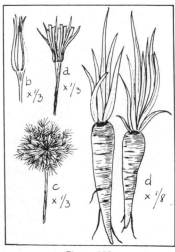

a, flowering head; b, head in bud; c, fruiting head; d, fleshy roots with leaves.

This plant, also known as Oyster Plant and Vegetable Oyster is a biennial reaching a height of some 3 feet when fruiting. The flowers are purple remaining open only during the forenoon.

The roots are white and foot long and 2 inches thick at the top. When cooked their flavor resembles that of oysters.

It is a native of Europe as is also YELLOW GOAT'S-BEARD, *T. pratensis* L, a worthless weed with pale yellow flowers.

145a Much curled leaves used for salads. Fig. 180 .... ENDIVE *Cichorium endivia* L.

Figure 180

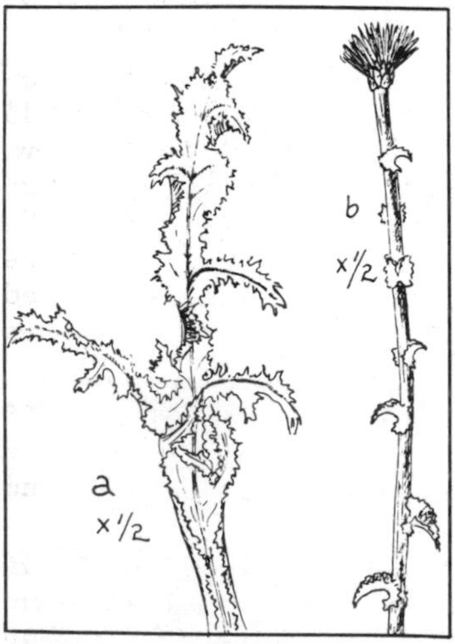

a, typical leaf; b, fruiting stalk with flowering head.

This plant is raised for its crisp curly leaves which are used in salads. The numerous young leaves grow in open heads and are marketed in that form. Later in the season a flowering stem arises to a height of 2 to 3 feet and produces composite heads with purple-rayed flowers.

The heads are often partly blanched by being covered for a time before cutting. It is known as "curly endive" in contrast to Witloof endive, which is a form of the next plant.

It is a native of India.

145b Stiff much branched plants, 1 to 4 feet high; stems yellow. The fleshy tap root used as a dilutant of coffee. Fig. 181..........
....................................CHICORY *Cichorium intybus* L.

a, fleshy roots; b, leaf; c, flowering stem with heads.

This plant has two chief food uses. The roots are dug after flowering, sliced, thoroughly dried, roasted with a little oil, and ground and mixed with coffee "to improve the coffee" or as an adulterant. It contains no caffein, but is said to make the coffee "go further."

The roots are also put in covered trenches for forced growth. The resulting white leaves are eaten as Witloof endive.

Chickory is a branching plant and grows to a height of 3 to 5 feet, with attractive azure-blue flowers, which has given it the name of Blue Sailors.

Figure 181

146a Plants 6 to 12 feet high, bearing harsh opposite leaves and producing edible tubers. Fig. 182...............................
..............JERUSALEM ARTICHOKE *Helianthus tuberosus* L.

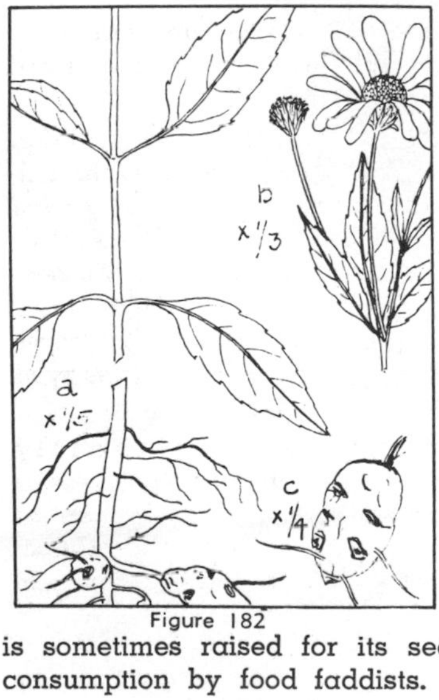

a, root with tubers and stem with leaves; b, branch with flowering head; c, tuber.

This is one of our native wild sunflowers. It grows to a height of 5-10 feet. The flowers are bright yellow. At its roots it produces solid club-shaped tuber sometimes reddish, others white. These tubers may be boiled, and eaten as potatoes, used in soups, or eaten raw as one eats radishes.

The food value is not high as the starch is not readily digested.

Other names are Girasole and Topinambour.

The COMMON SUNFLOWER *H. annuus* L., a closely related plant

Figure 182

is sometimes raised for its seed which is recommended for human consumption by food faddists.

146b Plants 3 to 5 feet high, bearing alternate leaves and fleshy flowering heads which are prized for food. Fig. 183 ....
.... GLOBE ARTICHOKE *Cynara scolymus* L.

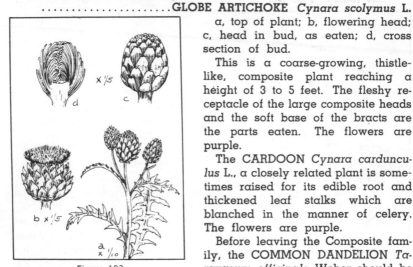

Figure 183

a, top of plant; b, flowering head; c, head in bud, as eaten; d, cross section of bud.

This is a coarse-growing, thistle-like, composite plant reaching a height of 3 to 5 feet. The fleshy receptacle of the large composite heads and the soft base of the bracts are the parts eaten. The flowers are purple.

The CARDOON *Cynara cardunculus* L., a closely related plant is sometimes raised for its edible root and thickened leaf stalks which are blanched in the manner of celery. The flowers are purple.

Before leaving the Composite family, the COMMON DANDELION *Taraxacum officinale* Weber should be mentioned, as it has been long valued as a spring tonic and is much used for greens. Its ragged-edged leaves are collected for this purpose. The flowers of this well-known plant are 1 to 2 in. in diameter and brilliant yellow.

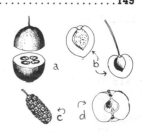

Figure 184

*Beginning at this place, the food uses of plants are employed as key characters. That results in many of the species appearing at two places in the key.

102

149a Plants with thick expanded leaf-like stems belonging to the Cactus family. Fig. 185......INDIAN-FIG *Opuntia ficus-indica* **Mill.**

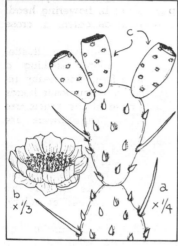

Figure 185

a, part of plant with fruit; b, flower; c, "pears."

Over 1000 species of the Cactus family are known. All are of American origin, although they have been carried to all parts of the world. All they possess in the way of leaves are some tiny scale like structures, the parts generally assumed as being leaves are stems. The fruit of the species, here pictured, is from 2 to 4 inches long and usually yellowish when ripe with the interior red. The pulpy contents is quite sweet and is intermingled with large seeds. This fruit is much depended on in Mexico and other regions. The young leaf-like stems have the thorns removed and are used for food.

The TUNA *Opuntia tuna* is another species the fruit of which is much used.

The flowers are yellow, and the fruit of the different species and varieties ranges in color from yellow to reds and purple.

152b Plants glabrous; stamens united in a tube and surrounding the stalk of the ovary. Stem sometimes somewhat woody. Fig. 186...
.............WILD **PASSION-FLOWER** *Passiflora incarnata* L.

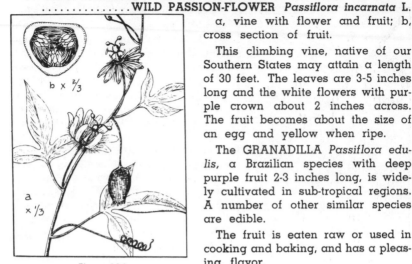

a, vine with flower and fruit; b, cross section of fruit.

This climbing vine, native of our Southern States may attain a length of 30 feet. The leaves are 3-5 inches long and the white flowers with purple crown about 2 inches across. The fruit becomes about the size of an egg and yellow when ripe.

The GRANADILLA *Passiflora edulis,* a Brazilian species with deep purple fruit 2-3 inches long, is widely cultivated in sub-tropical regions. A number of other similar species are edible.

The fruit is eaten raw or used in cooking and baking, and has a pleasing flavor.

Figure 186

153a Petals not united. Fig. 187a..
.........................**158**

153b Petals united. Fig. 187b....154

Figure 187

154a Flowers unisexual. Staminate flowers long, tubular, yellow with 10 stamens on throat, sepals small (pistillate flowers with distinct petals). PAPAYA **165b**

154b Both stamens and pistils in the same flower. Fig. 187.......155

155a With but one style......................................156

155b Styles two or more. Fig. 188.................................
..............COMMON PERSIMMON *Diospyros virginiana* L.

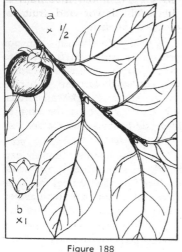

Figure 188

a, branch with fruit; b, flower.

This tree reaches a forest height of 50 feet or more, with leaves some 6 inches long; the fruit is yellowish or pinkish-orange when ripe and may be 1½ inches in diameter though usually smaller. It is exceedingly astringent when green, but becomes sweet, mild and delicious when fully ripened.

The JAPANESE PERSIMMON, *Diospyros kaki* L.f. bears orange or reddish fruit to 3 inches in diameter with excellent flavored orange colored flesh; often appears in the markets.

Ebony wood comes from the heart of a tree of this genus.

156a Flowers with sterile stamens (sometimes resembling petals)...157

156b Flowers with 5 fertile and no sterile stamens; fruit 2-4 in. in diameter, purple or light green. Fig. 189.......................
.......................STAR-APPLE *Chrysophyllum cainito* L.

Figure 189

a, branch with fruit; b, cross section through fruit showing seeds.

This tropical evergreen tree with 6 inch shining leaves grows to a height of 50 feet or more. The flowers are purplish-white and the spherical fruit which is about 4 inches in diameter is greenish to purple. The pulp is pinkish-white rather translucent and contains up to 8 brown seeds.

Many such tropical fruits are delightful but must be tree ripened and are poor keepers. Some of them are occasionally seen in our northern markets, but the public is often slow to accept new foods.

157a Sterile stamens petal-like, fruit rusty-brown, flesh yellow-brown. Fig. 190...................SAPODILLA *Sapota achras* Mill.

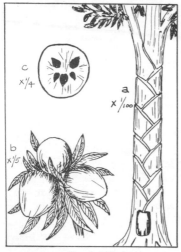

Figure 190

a, tree trunk groved for collecting chicle; b, fruit; c, cross section of fruit showing seeds.

This widely distributed tropical evergreen tree reaching 75 feet, has two distinct uses. The milky sap is collected boiled down and becomes the base (chicle) for most all of our chewing gums. It is interesting to note that the first use of chicle was for making rubber.

The 3 inch fruit with a rough yellowish-brown skin and translucent flesh of similar color with large shining black seeds is truly delicious. The flowers spread ½ inch and are white.

157b Sterile stamens only filaments, fruit orange-yellow, flesh dull orange. Fig. 191.............CANISTEL *Lucuma nervosa* A. D.C.

Figure 191

a, branch with fruit; b, cross section through fruit, showing seeds.

This slender tree 25 feet high with greenish-white flowers comes from tropical South America. Its leaves are bright green and 4 to 8 inches long. The fruit becomes 2 to 4 inches in diameter when mature. Its smooth, rather thin skin is bright orange in color. The flesh is mealy in texture and has a pleasing, distinctive flavor. One to five elongate, shining, dark brown seeds are imbedded in the flesh. Other names are Egg-Fruit and Ti-es.

159b Calyx not attached to the ovary; a very large tree; fruit covered with dense hair. Fig. 192........BAOBAB *Adansonia digitata* **L.**

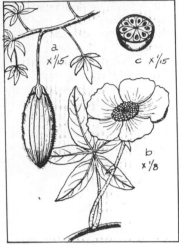

Figure 192

a, branch with fruit; b, flower; c, cross section of fruit.

This great African tree is also known as Monkey Bread and Sour Gourd, and is said to have the thickest trunk of any known tree although its height is only around 60 feet. It apparently grows to great age.

The fibrous bark is used for making clothes and rope while the acid-pulp fruit is eaten. The leaves when dried and powdered are used for seasoning.

The flowers are white and 6 inches or more across. Their stems are sometimes 3 feet long.

161a Young stems with four angles; veins of leaves conspicuous. Fig. 193.............................GUAVA *Psidium guajava* **L.**

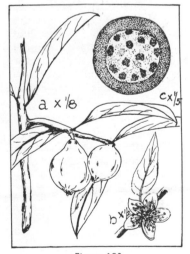

Figure 193

a, branch with leaves and fruit; b, flower; c, cross section of fruit.

Guavas grow on shrubs or small trees and while native of Tropical America are raised in the warmer parts of our Southern States. The fruit varies from spherical to pear shape and when ripe is pale yellow with white, yellowish or pink flesh. Guavas are prized for jellies, preserves, jams, etc.

Some enjoy eating them uncooked as they have a distinctive flavor. The fruit ranges from 1 to 4 inches in length. The center is thickly filled with seeds.

The flowers are white and about 1 inch across.

161b Young stems round in cross section; veins not prominent. Fig. 194.........STRAWBERRY GUAVA *Psidium cattleianum* **Sabine**

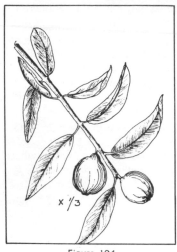

This fruit is smaller and with less flavor than the Guava but never-the-less is a favorite for jelly and jams in some regions. It grows on a shrub or small tree. The 1 inch flowers are white. The fruit 1 to 1½ inches in diameter, is purplish red with white flesh. One variety has bright yellow fruit. It is native of Brazil.

There are other species of Guavas, but not so well known as the two pictured.

Figure 194

162a Ovules hanging from tip of cell. Berry dark brown about ¼ inch in diameter. Fig. 195........ALLSPICE *Pimenta officinalis* **Berg.**

a, branch with fruit; b, panicle of flowers; c, flower.

This forty foot tree is a native of the West Indies and Central America. The leathery leaves are 6 to 7 inches long. The ¼ inch white flowers are borne in panicles. The berries that follow are picked before ripening and sundried. Since their flavor seems to resemble a mixture of several spices they have been called "Allspice."

Other names are Pimento and Jamaica Pepper.

The WEST INDIA BAYBERRY *Pimenta acris* Kostel is a similar. and closely related tree. An oil is distilled from the leaves to be made into bay rum.

Figure 195

162b Ovules not as in 162a.....................................163

163a With 3 to many flowers on each peduncle..................164

163b But one flower on each peduncle (though several peduncles may arise at the same place). Often a shrub. Fig. 196............
.................................PITANGA *Eugenia uniflora* L.

The fruit of this 25 foot shrub or tree is a crimson 1 or 2 seeded spicy-flavored berry nearly an inch in diameter. Its home is Brazil and Argentina. The fragrant flowers are about ½ inch across and white. Another name is Surinam-Cherry.

The JAMBOLAN *Eugenia jambolana* Lam. is a somewhat larger tree with small flowers and the branches white. Its half-inch berries are purplish-red. It is native of the East Indies.

Figure 196

164a Flowers ¼ inch across, light-purple. CLOVE TREE.........217a

164b Flowers 2 to 4 inches in diameter, greenish-white. Fig. 197......
.................................ROSE-APPLE *Eugenia jambos* L.

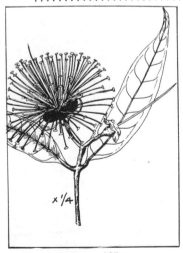

Here is another tropical evergreen tree, in this case only 30 feet high. It is native of the East Indies but is grown in our southern areas chiefly as an ornamental. The greenish-white flowers are 3 inches or more across with many conspicuous stamens, much outmeasuring the petals. The fruit is yellow and about 2 inches in diameter. Its flesh is rather dry and lacking in taste when eaten fresh, but is prized for preserves.

The AUSTRALIAN BUSH-CHERRY, *Eugenia myrtifolia*, Sims, is frequently grown as a hedge in warm regions. The 1 inch long red or purplish fruit is used in jellies.

Figure 197

165a Leaves simple, entire, glandular punctate; fruit globose, solid..166

165b Leaves up to 2 ft. across, blades as broad as long and much cut; fruit hollow with many spherical seeds. Fig. 198.............
..................................PAPAYA *Carica papaya* L.

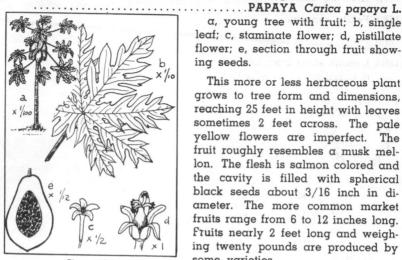

a, young tree with fruit; b, single leaf; c, staminate flower; d, pistillate flower; e, section through fruit showing seeds.

This more or less herbaceous plant grows to tree form and dimensions, reaching 25 feet in height with leaves sometimes 2 feet across. The pale yellow flowers are imperfect. The fruit roughly resembles a musk melon. The flesh is salmon colored and the cavity is filled with spherical black seeds about 3/16 inch in diameter. The more common market fruits range from 6 to 12 inches long. Fruits nearly 2 feet long and weighing twenty pounds are produced by some varieties.

Figure 198

The fruit is enjoyed both raw and cooked. Since it contains papain, a digestant acting as pepsin, the Papaya is the more popular. The seeds are often eaten as they are especially rich in papain. Commercial papain is extracted from the fruit.

166a Fruit when mature pale yellow (sometimes greenish) to red-orange; flowers when fully open, white, RUTACEAE..................96
166b Fruit reddish-purple; flowers 2 in. across, rose-pink; leaves 6 to 10 in. long. Fig. 199......MANGOSTEEN *Garcinia mangostana* L.

a, branch with leaves and fruit; b, fruit with part of covering removed showing fruit sections.

This 30 foot Malayan tree bears what is sometimes said to be the world's choicest fruit. The fruit, shaped like an orange contains 5 to 7 white segments and a few small seeds. The thick, tough rind is reddish-purple when ripe.

The flowers have a diameter of two inches and are rose-pink.

It would seem to have good possibilities once it is introduced into our markets.

Figure 199

167a Tropical shrubs 168

167b Growing naturally in temperate regions.....................170

168a Petals separate 169

168b Petals united. Leaves simple, entire, felt like, TREE-TOMATO.129a

169a Orange sized globular fruit filled with seeds each of which is surrounded by its own juicy pulp. Fig. 200.......................
.........................POMEGRANATE *Punica granatum* L.

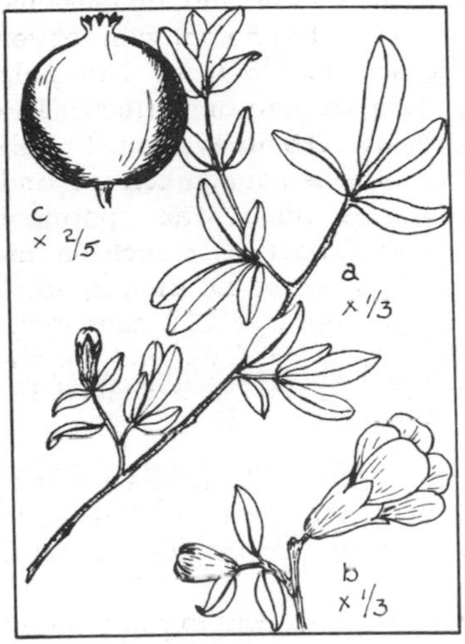

Figure 200

a, branch with leaves; b, bud and flowers; c, fruit.

This shrub (rarely a tree) grows to a possible height of 20 feet. The flowers are orange-red and waxy. The globular fruit 1½ to 4 inches in diameter contains several cells. Its many seeds are surrounded by a thick reddish, acid pulp. The fruit varies in color from pale yellow to pink, red and purplish-red.

Its chief use is in beverages and is more appreciated in hot dry climates. It has a long history but is not particularly popular.

Its quantity of seeds seem to be against it. A dwarf variety is raised as an ornamental pot plant.

169b Aromatic woody shrubs or trees not as in 169a. Family MYRTA-
CEAE 160

170a Leaves pinnately compound. Fig. 201a................171

170b Leaves simple. Fig. 201b..172

Figure 201

171a Fruit aggregate (a collection of drupelets). BRAMBLES...65

171b Fruit a 4 celled berry about ¼ inch in diameter. Fig. 202......
........................ELDERBERRY *Sambucus canadensis* **L.**

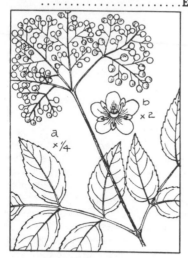

Figure 202

a, branch with fruit; b, single flower.

Several somewhat similar species of Elders are known. This one, known as the American or Sweet Elder is widely scattered east of the Rockies and its fruit was much used by early settlers and is still in use because of its flavor.

The bushes grow to a height of 10 to 12 feet. The flowers are borne in wide spreading umbel like cymes and are cream white. The fruit up to ¼ inch in diameter is purplish-black and is borne in great profusion.

The American Red Elder S. *pubens* bears bright red fruit which is somewhat poisonous.

172a Petals separate, on throat of calyx tube; fruit many seeded crowned with remains of calyx.............................173

172b Petals united...175

173a Stems with spines at nodes, flowers and fruit in groups of usually 1-4. Fig. 203.......GARDEN GOOSEBERRY *Ribes grossularia* **L.**

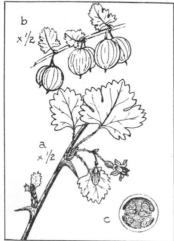

Figure 203

a, stem with flowers; b, fruit; c, cross section of fruit.

This is the European Gooseberry, the one generally planted for garden use. It is a shrub reaching a height of 2 to 5 feet. The berries may be an inch or more in length but are usually smaller and are very sour until ripened. The flowers are greenish or yellowish.

Several species of native gooseberries grow wild throughout our country and their fruit is often gathered and used. These native species are sometimes cultivated.

Gooseberries are used green more often than when ripe. They are alike in having thorns at the nodes and some species have prickles on the fruit.

112

173b Stems without spines at nodes, flowers and fruit in racemes. CURRANTS 174

174a Fruit black; leaves resinous-dotted. Fig. 204..................
..........................**BLACK CURRANT** *Ribes nigrum* L.

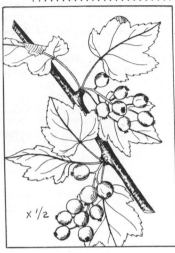

This is the European Black Currant a sturdy bush growing to a height of 5 feet or more, the fruit of which is used for jellies, preserves and the like. The flowers are greenish-white and the fruit is black.

The AMERICAN BLACK CURRANT *Ribes americanum* Mill. grows wild and bears similar fruit but it has an unpleasant flavor. Several varieties of *Ribes nigrum* are grown. They differ in the color of the ripened fruit and in the shape of the leaves.

The MISSOURI or BUFFALO CURRANT *Ribes odoratum* Wend. is planted for its golden yellow sweet scented flowers. One variety is grown for its fruit.

Figure 204

174b Fruit red or white (sometimes striped); leaves not dotted. Fig. 205
.....................**COMMON CURRANT** *Ribes sativum* Syme.

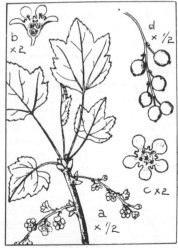

a, branch with flowers; b, section through flower; c, face view of flower; d, fruit.

This European shrub, common in many gardens, grows to a height of 3-5 feet. It bears many small greenish, yellowish or purplish flowers in hanging racemes. The fruit is a bright red or in some varieties, white. Currants are often used in cooking while still green. Currants are especially prized for jellies.

Several other European and native currants are known but are little planted with us.

Small seedless grapes when dried and used in baking are often referred to as "currants."

Figure 205

175a Stamens free from the corolla, leaves alternate; berries bluishblack or red...176

175b Stamens attached to the corolla, leaves opposite, plants to 12 ft. high; scarlet berries borne on cymes. Fig. 206..................
..................HIGH CRANBERRY *Viburnum trilobum* **Marsh.**

Figure 206

a, branch with fruit; b, section through flower; c, fruit.

This vigorous shrub may reach a height of 12 feet. The white flowers are borne in rather flat-topped umbel-like cymes, the outer ring of which has sterile flowers with large sepals, while the other flowers are much less conspicuous and fertile. The fruit is scarlet and eaten by birds. It may be used for jellies, etc.

The EUROPEAN CRANBERRY-BUSH, *V. opulus* L. often seen, is quite similar. One of its varieties is the Snowball (var. *roseum*) in which all the flowers are sterile, so it bears no fruit.

The BLACK-HAW *Viburnum prunifolium* L. has bluish-black fruit with large flat disk-like seeds. It is frequently eaten.

176a Fruit bluish-black with white bloom; flowers cylindrical; anthers not extending out of corolla................................177

176b Fruit red, flowers 4-parted open; anthers extending out of corolla. Fig. 207...AMERICAN CRANBERRY *Vaccinium macrocarpon* **Ait.**

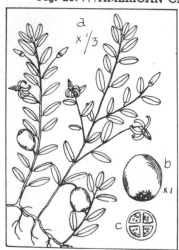

Figure 207

a, branch with leaves, flowers and fruit; b, single cranberry; c, cross section of fruit.

This woody evergreen has somewhat creeping stems 3 feet long. The leaves are less than an inch long and whitish beneath. The flowers are pink and about 1/3 inch across. The red fruit may be round, oval or pear shaped and is usually around ¾ inch long. Cranberries are raised in bogs which can be flooded at will. They are usually picked by use of comb-like scoops.

The EUROPEAN CRANBERRY *Vaccinium oxycoccus* L., a similar plant but smaller and bearing smaller fruit is sometimes raised.

177a Plants 4 to 12 ft. high, flowers pinkish or white. Fig. 208.......
............HIGH-BUSH BLUEBERRY *Vaccinium corymbosum* L.

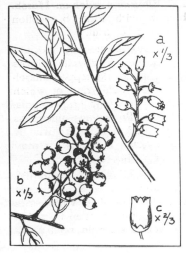

Figure 208

a, branch with leaves and flowers; b, fruit; c, single flower.

The shrubs may reach a height of 12 feet or more with leaves 3 inches long. The flowers are bell shaped about 1/3 inch long, pale pinkish. The bluish-black fruit is covered with a whitish bloom and is about 1/3 inch in diameter. It is later in fruiting than our other Blueberries.

There seems to be much confusion in the use of such names as Blueberry, Huckleberry, Whortleberry and Billberry. Other apparently good names for this plant are Swamp Blueberry and Huckleberry.

WINTERGREEN *Gaultheria procumbens* L., used for flavoring, is a closely related plant.

177b Plants seldom over 2 ft. high; flowers greenish white. Fig. 209..
............LOW BLUEBERRY *Vaccinium pennsylvanicum* Lam.

Figure 209

a, branch with fruit; b, flowering branch; c, single flower.

This somewhat prostrate little shrub grows to a length of 6 inches to 2 feet. The flowers are about 1/4 inch long and the bluish-black fruit which is usually covered with a bloom is 1/4 to 3/8 inch in size. It is among the first to ripen. Blueberries are often picked by use of a comb-scoop like that used with Cranberries. Leaves and sticks are then blown out.

Other similar plants whose fruit has food uses are HAIRY HUCKLEBERRY *Vaccinium hirsutum* native of Georgia and North Carolina, WHORTLEBERRY *Vaccinium myrtillus*, a Eurasian species with black fruit, and BLACK HUCKLEBERRY, *Gaylussacia baccata* Koch. a 3 foot deciduous shrub with black fruit.

178a Tropical vine; leaves broad, ovate, entire; fruit 1/4 in. in diameter or less, yellowish-red. PEPPER...........................197b

178b Tendril-climbing woody vines, leaves palmately lobed.......179

179a (b,c) Tendrils forked and intermittent (absent from each third
node). Fig. 210..............VINIFERA GRAPE *Vitis vinifera* L.

a, portion of vine with flower buds;
b, fruit.

This European grape is now raised
very extensively in California and to
some extent in other Southern States.
An aphid, the Grape Phylloxera and
mildew rule it out of other regions.
These Vinifera grapes are sweeter
than our American grapes and always favorites for table use. The
skin adheres to the pulp in contrast to
most of the American grapes.

Raisins are made by drying these
grapes, and from a small seedless
variety comes the so-called dried
currants used in baking.

There are many different varieties;
one var. *apiifolia* with much dissected leaves is raised as an ornamental.

Figure 210

179b Tendrils forked and continuous (at practically every node); bunches with many berries. Fig. 211...............................
................LABRUSCAN GRAPES *Vitis labruscana* Bailey.

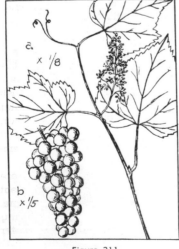

a, branch with leaves and inflorescence; b, fruit.

America has several species of
wild grapes. Some of these have
been improved by selection and
crossing with each other and with
the European grape until there are
many rather widely-differing varieties.

The Concord, derived from the
above species is likely the best
known and most widely raised east
of the Rockies. Its fruit is purplish
black with a whitish bloom. The
flowers are small and greenish yellow. Their petals fall as the buds
open. The flowers are borne in panicles. Other varieties derived from

Figure 211

this species take various shades of greenish-white and red when ripe.

They do not keep or ship as well as the Vinifera grape.

179c Tendrils not branching. Fig. 212..............................
................MUSCADINE GRAPE *Vitis rotundifolia* Michx.

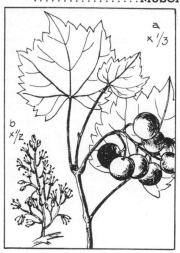

Figure 212

a, leaves and fruit; b, panicle of flowers.

The Muscadine is a southern grape. It has been broken into several varieties by cultivation and selection. The leaves are 2 to 6 inches across and smooth. The fruit is borne in small bunches of a very few to rarely 15 or 20 berries each, often ¾ to 1 inch in diameter.

"Scuppernong" a favorite variety bears fruit that when ripe is reddish-brown though often flecked with green. It is prized more for cooking and jellies than as a table grape.

The WINTER GRAPE *Vitis vulpina* L. is a common wild species the small black acid fruit of which is in strong favor for jellies.

180a Palm tree bearing its elongated drupe like fruit in great clusters.
    DATE PALM..31b
180b Not a palm 181
181a Native American shrub to 18 feet high, leaves 2 inches long, silvery both sides, drupes ¼ inch, red or yellow. Fig. 213........
    ....BUFFALO-BERRY *Shepherdia argentea* Nutt.

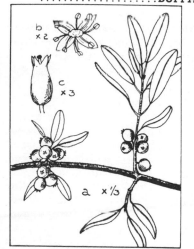

Figure 213

a, branch with fruit; b, staminate flower; c, pistillate flower.

This thorny 10-18 foot shrub is a native of the North and West. The young branches and leaves are matted with silvery hairs. The yellowish flowers are followed by little globular drupes that are red when ripe (var. *xanthocarpa* has yellow fruit). It is a very hardy shrub and is often employed for an attractive hedge.

The berries in earlier times were served as a sauce with buffalo meat which likely accounts for the name. They are prized for jelly making and are sometimes dried for winter use.

181b Not as in 181a..182

182a Flowers rose-like with many stamens arising from a ring surrounding the ovary. PLUMS, PEACHES, CHERRIES..........73
182b Not as in 182a..183
183a Trees with pinnately compound leaves....................184
183b Trees or shrubs with simple leaves......................186
184a Leaves odd pinnate with 3 to 11 leaflets; flowers brownish green; drupe, 1 inch long reddish. Fig. 214........................
..................................PISTACHIO *Pistacia vera* L.

This spreading deciduous tree attains a height of 25-40 feet. The flowers are brownish green and dioecious. The wrinkled reddish fruit is valued for its thin-shelled seed the yellowish or greenish meat of which is used in the making of candies and ice cream, or eaten directly and are known as Pistachio Nuts.

The tree is raised in ways similar to the Olive and in the same regions.

Figure 214

184b Leaves even pinnate with 2 to 4 pairs of leaflets............185

185a Surface of fruit smooth, green; flowers greenish-white. Fig. 215.
..........................SPANISH-LIME *Melicocca bijuga* L.

a, branch with fruit; b, inflorescence; c, staminate flower; d, pistillate flower.

This West India tree of some 60 feet has been introduced into the warmer areas of our southern states. The fragrant greenish-white flowers are borne in panicles. The drupe is about 1 inch in diameter with green skin and translucent yellow flesh. Both the flesh and the large seed are eaten, the latter being roasted.

It is also known as Mamoncello and Genip.

Figure 215

185b Surface of fruit roughened with tubercles, bright red. Fig. 216.
....LITCHI *Litchi chinensis* Sonn.

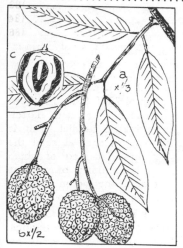

Figure 216

a, compound leaf; b, fruit; c, section through dried fruit.

This famous Chinese fruit or nut is now grown in many warmer regions. The round topped tree reaches a height of 30 feet or more, the small greenish-white flowers are borne in large panicles and are followed by a thin brittle shelled globular fruit which becomes a bright red upon ripening. The flesh is translucent, pinkish-white, sweet and aromatic.

The fruit is eaten fresh, used in preserves and dried as a confection. The tubercule covered shell of the dried "nuts" is a rust brown.

186a (b,c,d) Fruit globose 4-6 inches in diameter, russet, flowers white 1 inch. Fig. 217........MAMMEE-APPLE *Mammea americana* L.

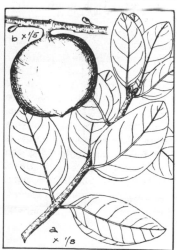

Figure 217

a, branch with leaves; b, fruit.

This beautiful tree of some 60 feet grows in tropical South America and the West Indies. The leathery leaves are a glossy green like many tropical evergreens. The white flowers are 1 inch across and fragrant. The globular fruit may attain a diameter of six inches. It has 1-4 large seeds imbedded in its bright yellow flesh. The somewhat roughened russet skin is bitter but the flesh is delightful either raw or in preserves. Its flavor has given it another name of South American Apricot.

186b Fruit variable shaped 2-6 inches long, greenish, yellowish or red-dish; leaves 6-16 inches long. Fig. 218 . . . .
. . . .**MANGO** *Mangifera indica* L.

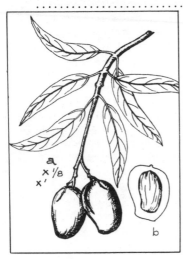

Figure 218

a, branch with fruit; b, fruit sectioned to show seed.

Likely of Asiatic origin the Mango justly famed for its delicious fruit is widely grown in tropical and near-tropical areas. The tree is a beautiful broad-spreading e v e r g r e e n which may attain a height of nearly 100 feet with a spread of 125 feet. The small pinkish-white flowers are borne in terminal panicles. The fruit varies in size from 2 to 6 inches and may be globular or elongated and yellow-green or red when ripe.

There are good and bad Mangos, the difference being much in the relative size of the seed and the quantity of fibers attach to it.

186c Fruit pear-shaped or globose 2 to 9 inches long, surface often roughened, green or purple. Fig. 219 . . . .
. . . .**AVOCADO** *Persea americana* Mill.

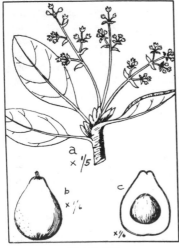

Figure 219

a, flowers and leaves; b, fruit; c, section of fruit showing seed.

This evergreen tree comes from Tropical America. It is very sensitive to frost which greatly limits the areas where it may be grown. The small freenish flowers are borne in panicles. The fruit which attains a length of 2 to 9 inches may be spherical or pear shaped. The color when ripe is usually green and sometimes purple, though there are brown and red varieties. The one large seed is surrounded by an oily pulp which is counted delicious by many.

The MEXICAN AVOCADO, variety *drymifolia*, has anise-scented leaves and smaller fruit.

186d Fruit smaller than in 186 a, b, or c 187
187a Drupe ½ to 1½ inch long, black when ripe; leaves 1-3 inches long, green above, silvery beneath. OLIVE 217b

187b Drupe 1½ to 2 inches long, dark red or brown, whitish flesh. Tree
or shrub; leaves 1-3 inches long, green, Fig. 220.................
....JUJUBE *Zizyphus jujuba* Mill.

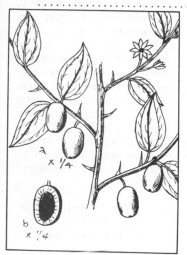

a, branch with leaves, flowers and
fruit; b, section showing seed.

This deciduous tree to 40 feet is
raised in the Mediterranean region
and in Asia, also in California and
Florida. The small flowers are whitish while the ½ to 1¼ inch long
fruit ranges in color from yellow to
red-brown and in some varieties
black. It is used much the same as
prunes or dates. The sugar content
is high.

Figure 220

188a (b,c) Vine with leaves two feet broad, much punctured; fruit
stands erect 6-12 inches (a monocotyledon). CERIMAN.......33b
188b Low growing plant with long spear-shaped leaves; fruit 3-10
inches long in center (a monocotyledon). PINEAPPLE.......44a
188c Not as in 188a or b...189
189a Flowers having no petals. Trees...........................190
189b Flowers with 6 petals. Calyx 3 parted. Trees..............191
190a (b,c) Fruit 4-8 inches in diameter; leaves 18 to 30 inches long.
Fig. 221.............BREAD-FRUIT *Artocarpus communis* Forst.

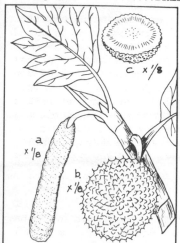

a, staminate spike; b, fruit; c,
cross section of fruit.

This tropical tree attains a height
of 60 feet. The large globular fruit
is covered with prickles and is yellow when ripe. Its contents is starchy
and it is usually cooked as a vegetable while still green. The fruit is
most often seedless so that suckers
and rootcuttings are employed for
propagation.

The natives make many uses of it.
The leaves are unusually large.

Figure 221

121

190b Flowers concealed within a pear-shaped receptacle which ripens to become the fruit. Fig. 222......COMMON FIG *Ficus carica* L.

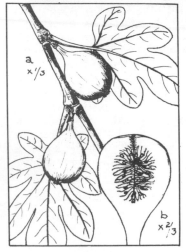

Figure 222

a, branch with leaves and fruit; b, section through fruit.

The fig is a peculiar plant in that its small flowers are always hidden within the fleshy receptacle which becomes the fruit. It is often said, it does not have flowers, but that is a mistake. The tiny wasps which pollinate the plant must crawl into the small opening at the end of the receptacle with their load of pollen or the many seeds which make the fig appreciated would not develop.

The tree may reach a height of 30 feet. The fruit is not a good keeper so while dried, preserved and canned figs are common, fresh ones do not travel far in quantities.

Several other species of the genus bear edible fruit and one of the Rubber trees and the Banyan are members of the genus.

190c Fruit resembling a blackberry ½ to 1 in. long. Fig. 223........ ....WHITE MULBERRY *Morus alba* L.

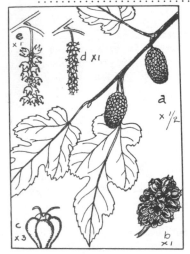

Figure 223

a, branch with fruit; b, fruit in detail; c, fruit of only one flower; d, catkin of pistillate flowers; e, staminate flowers.

These Chinese "white" mulberry usually bears red or purplish-black fruit, though occasionally white. It is the most common mulberry in many parts of our country, although its fruit is inferior in flavor to our native RED MULBERRY *Morus rubra* L. The White Mulberry is used for feeding silkworms but functions more largely with us in providing acceptable food for our native birds.

The BLACK MULBERRY *Morus nigra* L., a European favorite for its fruit, is sometimes grown here.

The fruit coarsely resembles blackberries but is derived from many flowers instead of but one as with the blackberry.

191a Fruit elongate, somewhat banana-shaped; seeds few. Fig. 224...
.............................PAWPAW *Asimina triloba* (L.)

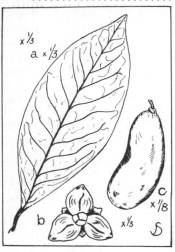

Shrub or small tree 10 to 35 feet in height. Young leaves and twigs clothed with a rusty down, becoming smooth as they mature. Flowers with 6 dull purplish petals, in groups of 3's (b). Fruit (c) 3 to 7 inches long, at first green but becoming brown at maturity; seeds somewhat flattened, imbedded in a sweet, edible pulp. Many nature lovers greatly enjoy this fruit. It is found in damp woods in the eastern half of our country. Frost seems to improve the fruit.

This member of the Custard Apple family is an example of a tropical plant that has moved north.

Figure 224

It is sometimes spelled "Papaw." This term, (either spelling) is also applied to the Papaya (see 165b) although the two plants are not related.

191b Fruit globular, scaly or muricate; seeds numerous...........192

192a Leaves velvety beneath. Fig. 225............................
.........................CHERIMOYA *Annona cherimola* Mill.

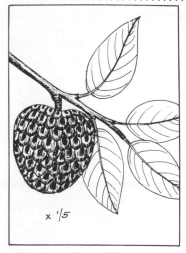

Ecuador and Peru have given this delightful fruit to the subtropics. The deciduous tree grows to a height of 25 feet; its leaves 10 inches long and its fragrant yellow to brownish flowers an inch across. The juicy fruit has a greenish exterior with white pulp and grows from apple size to specimens weighing 15 pounds. There are several varieties that differ in the shape of the fruit and type of surface.

The SOURSOP *Annona muricata* L., a 20 foot evergreen of Tropical America is closely related and bears similar fruit.

Figure 225

192b Leaves smooth beneath; carpels in fruit but loosely united. Fig. 226.......................SUGAR-APPLE *Annona squamosa* L.

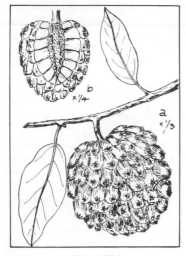

a, leaves and fruit; b, section through fruit.

This is another deciduous tree reaching a height of 20 feet and producing yellowish-green fruit about three inches in diameter. The flowers are greenish-yellow and about an inch long. It comes from Tropical America. The fruit is eaten both raw and cooked. Another name is Sweetsop.

The CUSTARD-APPLE *Annona reticulata* L. bearing heart-shaped reddish or brownish fruit up to 5 inches in diameter is similar.

Figure 226

197b Rather woody and net veined leaves; fruit small sessile globular berries. Fig. 227....................**PEPPER** *Piper nigrum* **L.**

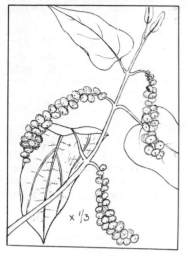

This tropical vining shrub is a native of India but is cultivated in Malaya and the East Indies. The berries are about ¼ inch or less in size and turn red when ripe. They are picked and dried just before ripening and often marketed in that form as "whole black pepper." If the outer covering is removed "white pepper" results.

CUBEB *Piper cubeba* L.f. produces similar berries which are used in medicine.

This pepper plant is not at all related or similar to the garden peppers, *Capsicum.*

Figure 227

198a Trees 25 feet or more high...............................**199**

198b Shrub or small tree 10-15 feet high bearing small red, 2-seeded berries. Fig. 228....................**COFFEE** *Coffea arabica* **L.**

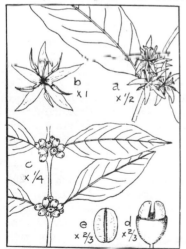

a, branch with flowers; b, single flower; c, branch with fruit; d, fruit dissected to show seeds; e, single seed

Coffee seems to have originated in Abyssinia and to have been prized as a beverage for many centuries. It is now raised in many tropical countries with Brazil being the largest producer.

The evergreen shrub has a height of 10 to 20 feet though in cultivation it is trimmed back for easy picking.

The flowers are a clear white and the pulpy berries bright red when ripe. The pulp is removed and the two seeds freed from a membranous coat. Roasting is a process that closely precedes marketing. No coffee is raised in the United States but 80% of the world's crop is consumed here.

Figure 228

At least two other species of this genus are known and used in similar way.

199a Fruit 5 inches or more in length..........................200

199b Fruit less than 2 inches in length; fruit and dried flower buds used as spice. CLOVES................................217a

200a Fruit large, ovoid, 5 ribbed, up to 1 foot long, growing from side of trunk and larger limbs. Fig. 229..CACAO *Theobroma cacao* L.

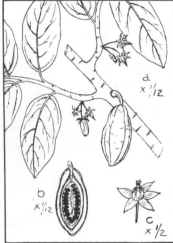

Figure 229

a, branch with leaves, flowers and fruit; b, section through a pod showing beans; c, a flower.

This 25 foot branching evergreen tree is native of Tropical America. The leaves reach a length of about a foot. The comparatively small pink flowers arise out of the stems, of the tree trunks in a rather unusual way. The fruit is an ovoid pod about a foot long. The seed, "beans," are attached to a central stem and are embedded in a soft pulp.

The beans are removed from the pods, washed, roasted, and ground in heated mills. The resulting product is the Bitter or Baking Chocolate. Much of the oil is removed to make Cocoa. Sugar and spices are added for other products.

200b Fruit 5-6 inches long. Kernels of the nuts used for drink. Fig. 230. ....COLA *Cola acuminata* S & E

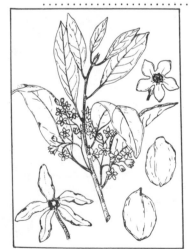

Figure 230

a, branch with leaves and flowers; b, flower; c, fruit; d, nuts.

These trees, reaching 40 feet in height are native of Tropical Africa but are now raised also in the American tropics. The leaves are 3-6 inches long. The rather small yellow flowers have no petals. One to 10 purplish nuts are enclosed in each brown pod (follicle). Five follicles usually arise from each flower.

The active principle is caffein as in Coffee. An extract from these nuts is thought to have a favorable influence on the digestive tract. It is much used in popular beverages most of which bear some modification of the "Cola" name.

201a (b,c,d) Fruit a legume. Fig. 231a...........................84a

201b Fruit a silique. Fig. 231b
.....................46a

201c Fruit a pair of usually,
ribbed a c h e n e s , and
borne in compound um-
bels. Fig. 231c......103a

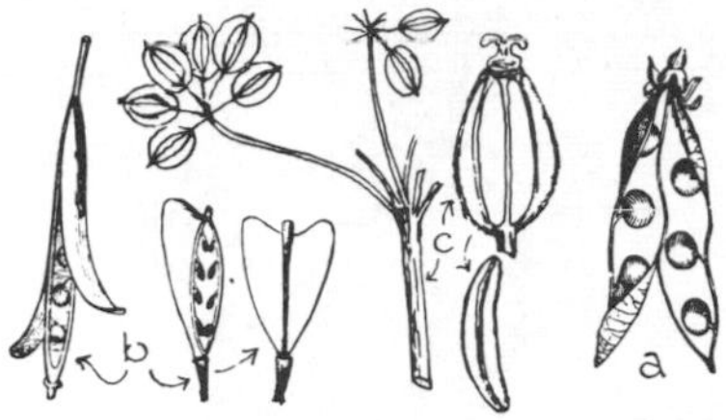

Fig. 231. Dry fruit. a, legume;
b, silique; c, schizocarp of 2 achenes.

201d Fruit not as in 201a, b or c................................202

202a (b,c) Succulent plants with peltate leaves. NASTURTIUM...232a

202b Harsh vines with soft cone like fruit. HOP...............221b

202c Not as in 202a or b.......................................203

203a (b,c) Plants coarse with large star shaped leaves and prickly fruit.
Fig. 232...................CASTOR-BEAN *Ricinis communis* L.

Figure 232

a, branch with flower panicle; b, section through fruit; c, seed.

A tropical tree 40 feet high which is raised as an annual with us. Its several-lobed peltate leaves may be 3 feet across. The flowering panicles may be 2 feet high with the pistillate flowers usually at the top and the staminate ones lower on the panicle. There are several varieties varying chiefly in color. Castor-oil is made from the seeds, hydraulic presses being used to extract the oil. Quantities of this oil is used in dyeing cotton goods.

Other names are Palma Christi and Castor-Oil-Plant. The plant is a native of Africa, but is raised all over the world for the seed or as an ornament. The seeds are poisonous to livestock.

203b Field plants to 3 feet high; flowers white; fruit a three sided, sharp pointed achene. Fig. 233...................................
...................BUCKWHEAT *Fagopyrum sagittatum* Gilib.

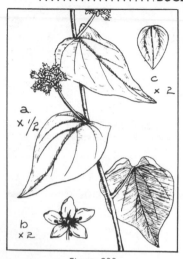

a, branch with leaves and flowers; b, single flower; c, three-sided seed.

This Siberian annual reached this country via Europe and is popular for making pan-cake flour. It grows to a height of 3 feet and produces a profusion of small, very sweet-scented, white flowers. The fruit is three angled and nearly black. Buckwheat flour contains more starch than that of the "small grains."

It is a favorite plant with bee raisers as it provides abundant nectar for a much prized honey.

Figure 233

203c Plants not as in 203a or 203b.................................204
204a Annual herbs, ovary after fertilization pushes under ground, where nut develops. PEANUT............................ ....87a
204b Annual herbs raised for the fiber surrounding the seeds and for the food oil in the seeds. COTTON........................245
205a (b,c) Shrubs with simple leaves. Fig. 234.....................
...............................FILBERT *Corylus avellana* L.

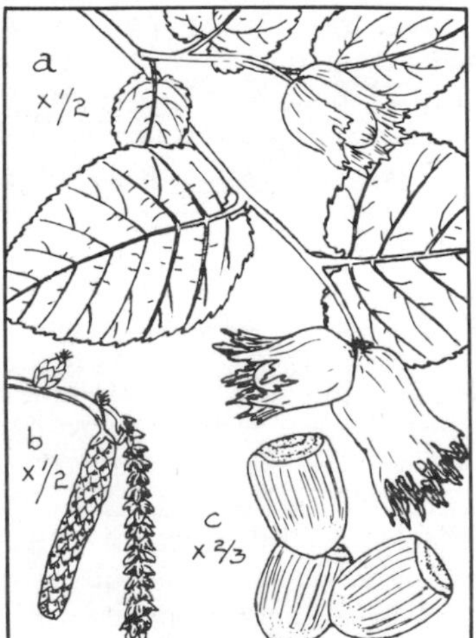

a, branch with fruit; b, flower catkins; c, nuts.

Several species of this genus produce closely similar nuts. They are shrubs or trees and are characterized by their long tassel-like staminate aments and the round or elongate brown nuts each borne in an enclosed husk.

The AMERICAN HAZLENUT *Corylus americana* Walt. grows wild in our Central and Eastern States.

Figure 234

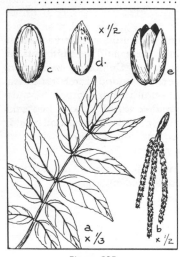

a, leaf; b, staminate flowers; c, fruit; d, nut; e, nut within the hulls.

This large growing hickory tree is native of the Mississippi valley as far north as southern Iowa. In recent years it has been greatly improved by breeding, and thin shelled varieties are now extensively raised commercially. They are coming into increased uses in pastries and for other food purposes.

Figure 235

207b Leaflets usually 3 to 5; nut flattened on two sides. Fig. 236.....
.....................SHAGBARK HICKORY *Carya ovata* Koch.

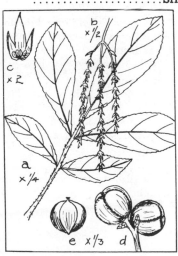

a, leaf; b, staminate ament; c, single staminate flower; d, fruit; e, nut.

This common forest tree, reaching a height of 120 feet, often produces quantities of hard shelled nuts of exceptionally good flavor. They and the nuts of several other similar species are gathered in the fall for home consumption or to put on the market.

The BIG SHELLBARK HICKORY *Carya lacinosa* Loud. grows nuts often more than an inch in length. The shell however is so thick and convoluted that it is difficult to remove the meat.

The nuts of several species such as the Bitternut and Pignut are too bitter to be edible.

Figure 236

129

208a Leaflets serrate; young twigs pubescent. Nuts rough and thick shelled 209

208b Leaflets almost entire; twigs glabrous. Nuts thin shelled and fairly smooth. Fig. 237........ENGLISH WALNUT *Juglans regia* **L.**

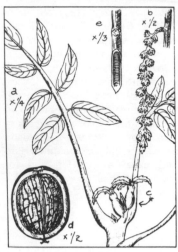

a, stem and leaves; b, staminate flowers; c, pistilate flowers; d, fruit with nut exposed; e, stem showing pith.

A native of South-eastern Europe and China this thin shelled nut is much raised in California and has a good market demand. The trees reach a height of 50 feet or more. The nuts are permitted to fall or are "polled" off, removed from the hull, cleaned, bleached and sorted before being put on the market.

Improved strains are perpetuated by grafting and budding.

Figure 237

209a (b,c,d) Fruit in long racemes covered with vicid hairs. Leaflets. 11-17, densely serrate. Fig. 238................................
.................JAPAN WALNUT *Juglans sieboldiana* **Maxim.**

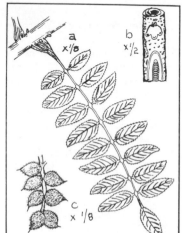

a, leaf; b, stem showing pith, and leafscar; c, fruit.

The nuts from this 60 foot tree are somewhat thinner shelled than Black Walnuts but not so thin as the English Walnuts. The nuts are pointed and borne up to 20 in each raceme. It is fairly hardy and is sometimes planted with us.

The CHINESE WALNUT *Juglans cathayensis* also bears pointed nuts about 2 inches long.

Figure 238

209b Fruit solitary or in pairs, almost spherical. Leaflets 15 to 23. Bark of larger limbs, dark and rough. Fig. 239.....................
..............................BLACK WALNUT *Juglans nigra* **L.**

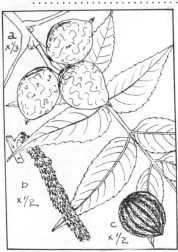

a, leaf and fruit; b, staminate flowers; c, nut.

This great 150 foot tree is of first importance because of its fine wood for furniture and other uses. Its nuts, however, have a distinctive much-liked flavor and are gathered for home use and market sale. The hull contains a penetrating and rather permanent brown stain, which marks the young walnut collectors each fall. The crank-turned type of corn-sheller offers a quick means of hulling the nuts.

Figure 239

209c Fruit elongate, in clusters of 3 to 5, coated with rust-colored sticky hairs. Leaflets 11 to 17. Bark of larger limbs with smooth light areas. Fig. 240.................BUTTERNUT *Juglans cinerea* **L.**

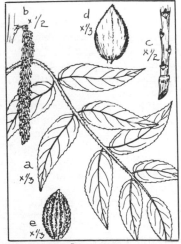

a, leaf; b, staminate ament; c, winter twig, showing leaf-scars; d, fruit; e, nut.

This tree is often called "White Walnut," presumably in reference to its light colored heart wood. The bark has smooth light patches in contrast to the rough dark bark of the Black Walnut. The leaves have from 11 to 17 leaflets and they and the fruit are covered with a sticky pubescence.

The nut meats are not as bulky as those of the Black Walnut and more difficult to get out of the shell. If the nuts are held on end when cracked, the meats may usually be gotten out much better.

Figure 240

209d Tropical or sub-tropical. Fruit a drupe, the seed known as PISTACHIO-NUT 184a
210a Native American trees; fruit a prickly nut; leaves with one fairly large simple serrate tooth for each lateral vein, in which it ends 211

211a Leaves with slender points on the teeth often incurving. Leaves more than twice as long as wide, green on both sides. Bark rough. Fig. 241...........CHESTNUT *Castanea dentata* Borkh.

a, branch with staminate flowers; b, fruit (burs) with nuts; c, chestnut.

This native American tree grows to a height of 100 feet and has leaves 10 inches long. Its 2-3 nuts are grown in a very prickly bur which breaks open in the fall and pours out the nuts. They are one inch or less across. Chestnut Blight has practically eradicated our native chestnuts from their natural area.

The CHINQUIPIN *Castanea pumila* Mill is another native species which bears similar but smaller nuts of excellent flavor.

Foreign Chestnuts are the Eurasian, Chinese and Japanese, all of which have nuts larger, but inferior in flavor to our American species.

Figure 241

Chestnuts are much used as a substitute for grain in some old world regions.

211b Leaves without slender points at tips; usually less than twice as long as wide. Bark smooth, light gray. Several 3-sided nuts borne in the spiny fruit. Fig. 242......BEECH *Fagus grandifolia* Ehrh.

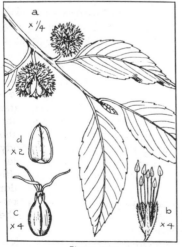

a, branch with leaves and fruit; b, staminate flower; c, pistillate flower; d, seed.

Beech nuts grow in very prickly burs much the same as chestnuts; the nuts however are three angled and smaller. They would appear to be overgrown buckwheat grains. Their sweet-flavored kernels give them good food value.

The tree grows to a height of 100 feet and has smooth light gray bark and beautiful lustrous green foliage.

The EUROPEAN BEECH, *Fagus sylvatica* L. is often planted with us as an ornamental. There are different colors of foliage and cut-leaf and "weeping" forms. The nuts are similar to those already described.

Figure 242

212a Trees peach-like, fruit a drupe, its fleshy covering splitting early. The seed constitutes the "nut." **ALMOND**...................75b
212b Not peach-tree-like 213
213a Receptacle becoming fleshy and forming the largest part of the fruit; supporting a curved nut at its end. Fig. 243...............
...........................**CASHEW** *Anacardium occidentale* L.

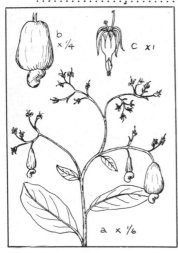

a, branch bearing flowers and fruit; b, fruit; c, flower.

This 40 foot, wide-spreading tropical evergreen yields both fruit and nuts in the same package. A large fleshy pear-shaped body with pleasing acid pulp is first on the pedicel, then at its apical end, as though Nature just noticed that the seed had been forgotten, is attached the familiar cashew nut. The "cashew-apple" turns red or yellow when ripe. It is 2 to 4 inches in length and is eaten raw or used for beverages and other foods.

The nuts are eaten both raw and roasted, but when raw must be handled with care for within the shell is a caustic blistering liquid which heat dispells.

Figure 243

The flowers are yellowish-pink and about ½ inch long.
213b Receptacle normal 214
214a Fruit a woody shelled sperical ball 3 to 5 inches in diameter enclosing several close fitting U sided nuts. Fig. 244.............
.....................**BRAZIL NUT** *Bertholletia excelsa* H. & B.

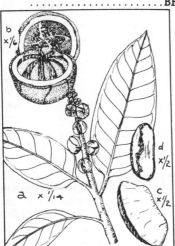

a, flowering branch with leaves; b, fruit cut open to show nuts; c, a typical nut; d, kernel from nut.

This 150 foot tree, native of northern South America, is scarcely known outside its own region except by its nuts. The leaves are leathery and about 2 feet long, the flowers are cream colored and the spherical fruit, with thick woody wall, reaches 6 inches in diameter. The fruit wall is broken with difficulty. Inside are 18 to 24 triangular nuts, each with one large fleshy kernel, in taste resembling that of the coconut.

Other names are Para-nuts, Castanea and Cream-nut.

Figure 244

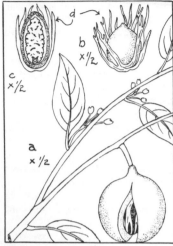

Figure 245

a, branch with leaves, flowers and fruit (flesh cracking to expose nuts); b, nut surrounded by aril (mace); c, section through nut; d, covering of nut (mace).

This tree, a native of the East Indies may attain a height of 60 feet or more, but the trees in cultivation are usually kept cut back to about 25 feet. The leaves are 2-5 inches long, the flowers are inconspicuous and the fruit yellowish or reddish, up to 2 inches in diameter. The outer fleshy covering is removed; under it and surrounding the nut is a scarlet lacework which is dried and marketed as the spice, Mace.

The nuts are dried until the kernel shrinks away from its enclosing shell, which is then removed. This dry kernel is the Nutmeg used as a spice in cooking.

Figure 246

a, leaves, buds and flowers; b, section of flower; c, fruit.

This is a beautiful evergreen tree growing to a height of 30 feet with leaves about 3 inches long. Twice a year it produces a profusion of red or purplish flowers. The flower buds are picked and dried to furnish our cloves as they appear on the market. Cloves are now produced in the East Indies, Zanzibar and British East Africa.

ALLSPICE *Pimenta officinalis* Berg. a closely related 40 foot tree with white flowers, produces the small brown fruit which when dried immature, gives us this spice. (See 162a).

217b Leaves silvery beneath; green or ripe drupe fruit pickled. Fig. 247................................**OLIVE** *Olea europaea* **L.**

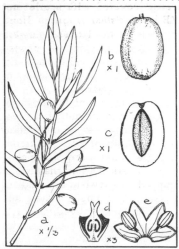

a, branch with fruit; b, an olive; c, section of fruit showing seed; d, section of pistilate flower; e, section of staminate flower.

This is a most important tree of 25 feet or more, in the Mediterranean region and in California and Arizona. The leaves are 1-3 inches long, densely covered with silvery scales on under side. The flowers are white and very fragrant. The fruit grows to a length of ½ to 1½ inches and is shining dark purplish-brown when ripe. The trees live to a very old age, — perhaps as much as 2000 years.

From 10 to 30% of the flesh of the fruit is oil, which is rather readily extracted and finds a good market.

Figure 247

Both green and ripe olives are pickled in brine or vinegar, with or without spices.

218a (b,c) Fruit a legume, flowers pea-shaped.....................85
218b Leaves peltate, flowers with a spur. NASTURTIUM........232a
218c Not as in 218a or 218b...................................219
219a Abnormal buds or flowers developing into a fleshy head surrounded by cabbage-like leaves............................53
219b Fruit an elongated, five-sided capsule filled with shot-like seeds. Fig. 248..........................**OKRA** *Hibiscus esculentus* **L.**

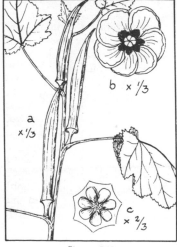

a, branch with fruit; b, flower; c, cross section of fruit showing seeds.

This plant is a near relative of the Hollyhock and of Cotton. It grows from 2-8 feet high. Its large leaves may measure a foot or more across. The flowers are pale yellow with a reddish center and are followed by elongated pods ranging in length from 3-12 inches. These pods become tough and woody when they mature but while young and tender are much prized throughout our South.

They have a gummy contents and are used in soups, stews and as a vegetable. The seeds are sometimes roasted and used as a substitute for coffee. Another name is Gumbo.

Figure 248

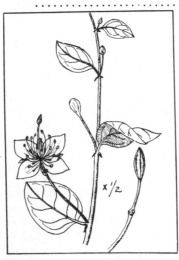

This spiny perennial shrub, growing to a height of some 3 feet belongs in the warmer Mediterranean regions, but is sometimes raised as an annual farther north. The leaves are 1-2 inches long. The flowers are white and have a spread of 1½ to 2 inches with many long stamens.

The flower-buds are picked from mid-summer until fall, dried, and then pickled in brine or vinegar to which various spices are added. Before marketing the "Capers" are run through sorting sieves to grade the buds by size. The smaller ones are valued most.

Nasturtium fruits are sometimes mixed with the Caper buds to cheapen the pickles.

Figure 249

a, staminate flowers and leaves; b, pistillate flowers; c, fruit.

This rough stemmed twining vine with 3-5 lobed leaves and small greenish-white flowers often grows as an escape in our country. The root is perennial but the vine dies each year. The multiple fruit is somewhat similar to that of the Mulberry to which it is related except that each ovary is covered with a large leaf-like bract giving the fruit a leafy cone appearance.

Hops are used in some beverages to impart a bitter taste and to retard bacterial action. The tender young shoots are sometimes eaten the same as Asparagus.

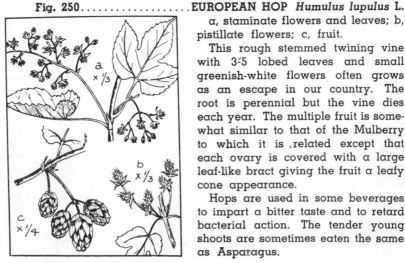

Figure 250

The so-called AMERICAN HOP *Humulus americanus* Nutt. with 5-11 lobed leaves, is similar in growth and uses, and questioned as a valid species.

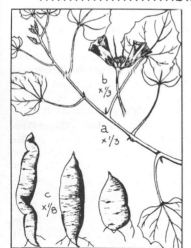

a, vine; b, flowers; sweet potatoes of different shapes.

This plant grows from thick fleshy roots which are found rather deep underground. The funnel-shaped flowers, 1½ to 2 inches long are bluish, rose-violet or pale pink. It is a native of tropical America. There are many cultivated varieties, some of which are known as yams. True yams, however, belong to the genus *Dioscorea*. (See 42a)

Sweet-potato plants are raised by placing the fleshy roots in hotbeds in early spring. Numerous sprouts appear. These rooted young plants are removed when 3 to 6 inches long and set out in ridged rows. The tubers continue to grow new plants,

Figure 251

a bushel of tubers yielding 3000 to 4000 plants.

The sugar contents ranges from 4 to 10%, 100 bushels per acre is a good yield, although much greater yields are frequently raised.

223b Herbaceous tropical shrub to 9 feet high. Fig. 252..............
.................TAPIOCA-PLANT *Manihot esculenta* Crantz

a, branch with deeply lobed leaves and flowers; b, pistillate flower; c, staminate flower; d, root.

This native of Brazil is a highly important food plant. The fleshy roots are ground and the starch washed out and then heated until the starch grains explode. This mass is then made up into various forms for marketing. Tapioca is used for puddings, soups, etc. The natives grate the roots, and make bread from this plant.

The Tapioca-plant is sometimes grown from seed, when raised commercially, but the more common practice is to plant pieces of the stem in much the same way as with sugar cane. In regions subject to frost the canes are buried until spring, and are then cut into lengths of about 5 inches for planting. The roots do not keep well after being dug so they are allowed to remain in the ground until processing is ready.

Figure 252

Other names are Manioc and Cassava.

224a Herbaceous plant to 3 feet high, tubers usually smooth with prominent eyes, flowers starshaped. POTATO...................123a

224b Sunflower-like plants 6-10 feet high; tuber usually hard and rough. JERUSALEM ARTICHOKE.........................146a

225a Plants with milky sap; flowers daisy-like, blue or lavender...144

225b Flowers not daisy-like......................................226

226a (b, c) Flowers with 4 separate petals, fruit a silique.........46a

226b Flowers with 5 petals borne in simple or compound umbels; fruit dry separating into two parts..............................103a

226c Garden or field plants with globular or elongated fleshy tap roots; leaves entire or sinuate; flowers small, greenish or reddish. Fig. 253.....................................BEET *Beta vulgaris* **L.**

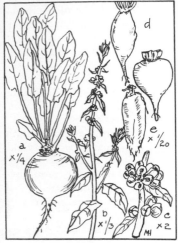

a, typical beet plant; b, flowering branch; c, flowers; d, root shapes; e, sugar beet.

This well known plant takes a number of forms and finds several uses. It is ordinarily a biennial and reaches a height of 2-4 feet when in bloom. The flowers are small and greenish or reddish.

Table Beets are usually deep red and the roots comparatively small. Sugar Beets, on the other hand, are nearly white, often weighing several pounds each and have a sugar content of 10% or more.

It is one of the world's largest sources of sugar with a yield of 13,010,000 tons in our country in 1956. It is exactly the same as cane

Figure 253

sugar with the possible exception of any scant bits of impurities peculiar to the plant tissue from which the sugar comes.

The leaves of beets are cooked as greens. SWISS CHARD belongs here (see Fig. 268).

The Mangels, large coarse growing beets, are used as stock feed.

227a (b,c) Tree; bark of roots used for beverage, flavoring and spring tonic. Fig. 254............SASSAFRAS *Sassafras albidum* **Nees**

a, shoot with leaves and fruit; b, spring twig with flowers; c, staminate flower; d, pistilate flower; e, "mitten" leaf.

This tree may attain a height of 60 feet. The occasional two-lobed leaves have won for it the name "Mitten Tree." The flowers are small, bright yellow and appear before the leaves. The fruit is blue with red pedicels. The twigs are yellowish-green and all parts of the tree aromatic.

The twigs, leaves and buds are sometimes used to thicken and flavor soup. These parts, or more often the bark of the roots, are used in making "Sassafras tea," popular as a spring tonic or even as a substitute for regular tea.

Figure 254

The tree also figures in the manufacture of candy, perfumery and dyes.

227b Large tree with sharply serrate leaves (a), aromatic. Fruiting with catkins (b). Fig. 255 . . . .**SWEET BIRCH** *Betula lenta* L.

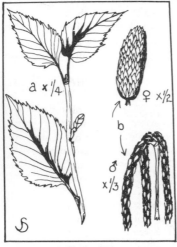

This tree, rather common in our eastern states, may attain a height of 80 feet. The leaves are glossy bright green above and dull green below. The twigs and leaves when boiled and distilled yield oil of wintergreen, much used in food flavoring and also in medicine.

There are several, rather small, true wintergreen plants which yield this same oil but in lesser quantities.

Much of the oil of wintergreen now in use is made synthetically.

Figure 255

227c Tree; bark from branches used as spice. Fig. 256 . . . .
. . . .**CINNAMON-TREE** *Cinnamomum zeylanicum* Breyn.

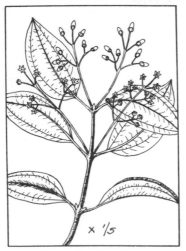

This stiff-leaved evergreen tree grows to a possible height of 30 feet, but in cultivation is kept cut back to a few feet so that quick growing shoots are produced. These are cut when about an inch in diameter, the bark removed to loosen it, then put back in place for a few hours of fermentation. When again removed the outer part is scraped away leaving the inner bark which is then curled into a roll as stick cinnamon.

This, the original cinnamon is produced in Ceylon. Most of the cinnamon on the market is similarly produced from the CASSIA-BARK-TREE *Cinnamomum cassia* Blume., a native of China but much raised in the East Indies.

Figure 256

The CAMPHOR-TREE is a species *camphora* N. & E. of this same genus.

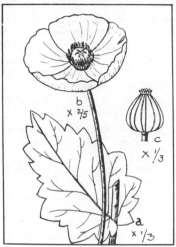

Figure 257

a, stem-leaf; b, flower; c, fruit (capsule).

This plant likely has scant claim to be included in a food book. It is a usually glaucous annal 2-4 feet high with leaves 4-10 inches long and red or purplish flowers 3 inches or more across. The fruit is a salt-shaker-type of capsule.

In making opium the milky juice from the slit capsules is collected, dried and processed. The plant is common with us as an ornamental and as a frequent escape. India, Persia and China have been the outstanding poppy raising regions.

Figure 258

a, trees tapped for sap; b, leaves and seeds of Black Maple.

Maple sugar was once the principal sweetening for table use and in cooking. It is still made and marketed and is used in candy making. Maple syrup seems to "belong" with pancakes.

Perennials store much reserve foods in roots and stems over winter. As spring approaches these foods are transported as a sugar solution to the growing parts of the plant to aid in quick growth.

The sap of several species of maples have a good sugar content —often 4% or better—and a pleasing flavor. Man long ago learned to tap the trees, collect the sap and by boiling out the water, to make sugar or syrup. Several species of Maple trees may be thus used. The one here pictured is *Acer nigrum* Michx.

229c Large grass-like plants with solid pith containing sweet juice..230

230a Nodes (joints) far apart; grows throughout our country. SWEET SORGHUM 20a

230b Nodes close together; semi-tropical or tropical. SUGAR CANE..19b

231a Plants with composite flowers; several to many flowers united in a compact head surrounded by a whirl of bracts..........141a

231b Flowers not composite....................................232

232a Leaves peltate (petiole attached within the margins of the blade). Fig. 259.........GARDEN NASTURTIUM *Tropaeolum majus* L.

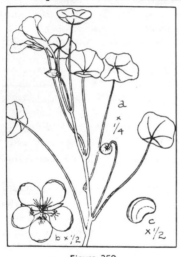

Figure 259

a, branch of plant; b, face view of flower; c, fruit.

This annual, with us, is a perennial in tropical America where it is native. The peltate leaves 2-6 inches across and the bright yellow, orange or red flowers characterize the plant. Our excuse for showing it here is the occasional use of its stems and fruit to season relishes, pickles, etc. The seeds are pickled much the same as Caper buds. The plant is ordinarily of vining habit.

There are a number of species within the genus;—a dwarf bushy form, *Tropaeolum minus* L., being often raised.

Tropaeolum tuberosum R. & P. grows irregular cone-shaped tubers 2-3 inches long which are eaten in South America.

232b Leaves not peltate..233

233a Flowers without petals......................................237

233b Flowers with petals...234

234a Petals united into a tubular corolla. Fig. 260a 236

234b Petals not united to each other. Fig. 260b 235

235a (b,c) Petals four, fruit a silique..46a

Figure 260

235b Petals 5, usually small, in compound (rarely simple) umbels..103a
235c Petals and stamens 4; fruit a berry. A native of Brazil and Para-
guay. Fig. 261..............MATE *Ilex paraguayensis* **St. Hil.**

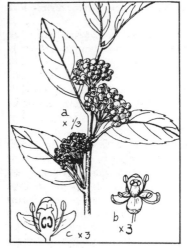

Figure 261

a, branch of plant with fruit; b, flower; c, section through a flower.

This shrubby holly plant is widely cultivated in Brazil. It is a broad-leaved evergreen bearing cluster of small flowers and later, red berries.

Its leaves (the young partly-grown ones are best) are collected, dried for 24 hours and then broken into small pieces for tea making.

The plant contains both caffeine and tannin in about the same proportions as coffee but since less of it is used to make a serving, Mate tea contains less of these stimulants than coffee. It is served very hot and with sugar, cream or lemon as one wishes, much as ordinary tea.

It has been long used in South America and its export to our country has been increasing.

236a Corolla, irregular, usually two lipped. Stems square; strongly
flavored plants 115a
236b Corolla regular with 5 white petals and many stamens. Leaves
used as a beverage. Fig. 262..............TEA *Thea sinensis* **L.**

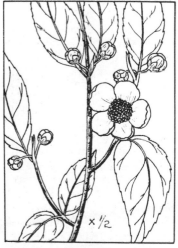

Figure 262

The use of tea as a beverage seems to date back nearly 5000 years; it has the largest use of any beverage.

The plant is an evergreen shrub or tree growing to a height of 30 feet. The leaves are from 3 to 8 inches long. The white, fragrant flowers are 1 to 1½ inches across.

Like most of the other important cultivated plants, it runs to many varieties.

The trees are started from seed and set out permanently when quite small. They may be picked at 4 years of age. They are cut back to a height of two feet to produce quick growing shoots ("flushes") with tender leaves. The young leaves are picked by hand, then processed, sorted and packed. Black and green tea come from the same plant. In making black tea the leaves are fermented before drying.

237a Ovary with but one cell and one seed......................238
237b Ovary with several cells each producing one seed. Fruit with hard wall, indehiscent. Fig. 263...............................
.......**NEW-ZEALAND-SPINACH** *Tetragonia tetragonioides* Ktze.

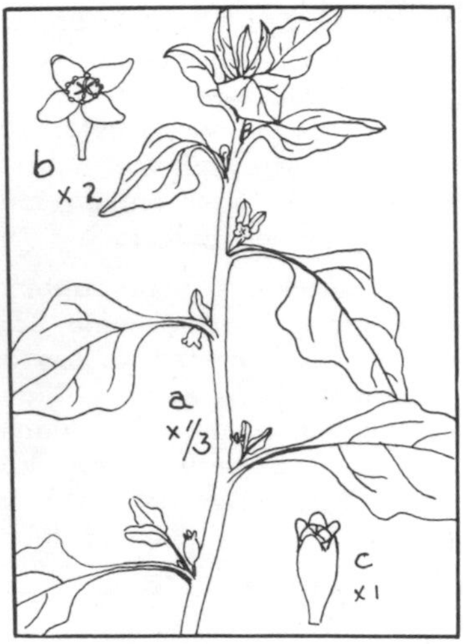

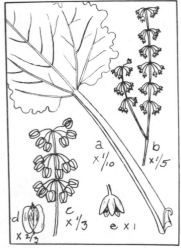

a, branch with leaves and fruit; b, flower; c, fruit.

Ordinary spinach does not do well in warm weather. It is at that time that New-Zealand-Spinach becomes most useful. While not so well liked as ordinary spinach, this sturdy grower produces a good crop the whole summer through.

It is a strong growing, prostrate annual with leaves 2 to 5 inches long and 2 or 3 small yellow-green flowers in each leaf axil. The top-shaped fruit is about 1/3 inch long and woody. The fresh young branches and leaves are the parts cooked. It readily reseeds itself.

It is native of South America, New Zealand, Australia and Japan.

Figure 263

238a Young stems with sheath at nodes. Fruit dry, with 3 wings...239
238b Young stems without sheath at nodes......................241
239a Stamens 6. Sheath often falling off as stems mature........240
239b Stamens usually more than 6; leaves large with heavy, juice-filled petioles. Sheath prominent and persistent. Fig. 264............
....................**GARDEN RHUBARB** *Rheum rhaponticum* L.

a, part of leaf; b, flowering branch; c, fruiting branch; d, single fruit; e, single flower.

This Old World perennial often called "Pie-Plant or Wine-Plant" is widely raised and justly famed for its acid juice.

The leaves grow from fleshy roots and may be pulled at any size. The leaf blade is discarded and the reddish petiole stripped of its outer skin, cut into pieces and stewed.

Presently a heavy flower stem arises to a height of 4-6 feet. This is usually removed early to conserve the strength of the roots. The flowers are greenish yellow followed by brown seeds.

Figure 264

144

240α Plants slender with hastate leaves. Fig. 265.................
.........................GARDEN SORREL *Rumex acetosa* L.

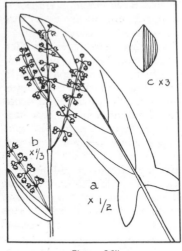

a, leaf; b, flowering branch; c, seed.

This plant along with others of its family, finds use as spring greens. When fruiting, it attains a height of 3 feet. Its leaves are about 5 inches long and mostly radical; with thin, light green blades and long petioles.

The yellowish-green unisexual flowers are borne on thick panicles. It is a native of Asia and Europe.

The so-called French or Belleville spinach is a variety of this species.

Figure 265

240b Plants heavier; leaves 12 to 15 inches long, not hastate. Fig. 266.
.........................SPINACH-DOCK *Rumex patientia* L.

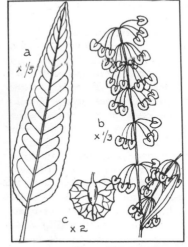

a, leaf; b, branch with fruit; c, seed.

This perennial often known us Horb Patience, is frequently seen growing as an escape with us. Europe is its native home. The root leaves are cooked as greens either by themselves or with Spinach or other plants. The Docks have a pleasing acid.

Its heavy flowering panicle rises to a height of 5 or 6 feet and bears abundant flowers and fruit. The leaves are usually over a foot long and somewhat curled.

Figure 266

241α Flowers perfect. Plants either with fleshy taproot or with large petiole **242**

145

241b Flowers imperfect. Plants 6 inches to 2 feet high; seeds enclosed in a more or less spiny body. Fig. 267.........................
.............................SPINACH *Spinacia oleracea* L.

Figure 267

a, young plant; b, fruit; c, fruit of Round-seeded variety.

In recent decades Spinach has been much exploited on account of its mineral and vitamin contents. In Texas and other market crop areas where it is grown on a large scale the acreage has increased many fold. It is a cool weather plant, so does not do well when warmer days are with us.

In fruit, it reaches a height of 2 feet and has yellowish-green flowers, followed by prickly 2 to 4 seeded fruit. ROUND-SEEDED SPINACH var. *inermis* differs in having no spines on the fruit.

ORACH *Atriplex hortensis* L. is a closely related plant, occasionally raised for similar use.

242a With fleshy, usually globular taproots; leaves as well as root eaten. GARDEN BEET....................................226c

242b Petiole and midrib of leaves heavy and succulent. Fig. 268......
.......................SWISS CHARD *Beta vulgaris* var. *cicla* L.

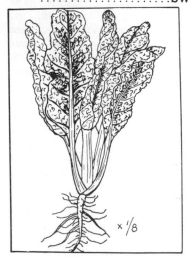

Figure 268

This is just a variety of the Beet which does not have a fleshy root. The reserve food is stored in the leaves which possess heavy midribs and make them prized as pot-herbs. The plant grows vigorously from early summer until frost and is an abundant food producer of its kind. Some Leaf Beets with colored leaves are grown as ornamentals.

Seeds are produced, as with beets, by keeping the plant over winter and setting it out the second spring when it will flower and fruit. It's easier for the home gardener however just to get his seed at the corner grocery.

PLANTS YIELDING FIBERS, JUICES OR PIGMENTS*

245a (b,c) Seeds with extra long fibers (lint) but without a short woolly covering (smooth when lint is removed at the gin). Flowers bright yellow with purplish tinge. Many of the leaves 5-lobed. Fig. 269. ....SEA-ISLAND COTTON *Gossypium barbadense* L.

Figure 269

a, plant with flower and boll; b, seed with fiber; c, seed as it comes from the gin.

This cotton plant grows to a height of 3-8 feet. The natives of the West Indies were using it when Europeans first visited the islands. The lint is finer and longer (1⅜-2 inches) than that of Upland Cotton, so brings a considerably better price, but its yield is less and the cost of harvesting more. It is now raised along the coast of Georgia and Florida as well as in several of the West India Islands.

The use of fibers from the seeds of cotton dates back at least 3000 years. Many changes from hybridization, selection, etc., have occurred.

A good number of species and many varieties are now recognized but botanists are not well agreed on it all. It is one of man's most important plants.

*A few of these plants are Monocotyledons and have already been pictured and described in that section on the earlier pages of the book. They are included in this key also to keep the fiber list intact. At most, the number of plants thus used is surprisingly small. Man draws as further source for fibers on some animals and in a smaller way on the minerals. Then an ever increasing amount of fibers and pigments are being manufactured synthetically. For some of these, plant materials furnish the base, while coal, petroleum and other organic compounds serve as the starting point for other synthetic fibers.

245b Seeds with shorter fibers, and covered with short woolly hairs after ginning; flowers white or pale yellow turning pink or purplish. Leaves 3-lobed. Fig. 270 ....
...................UPLAND COTTON *Gossypium hirsutum* L.

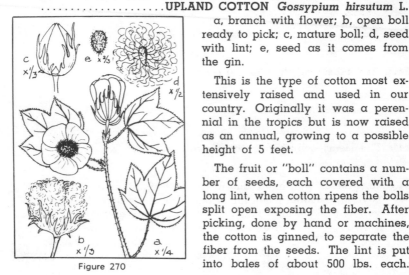

Figure 270

a, branch with flower; b, open boll ready to pick; c, mature boll; d, seed with lint; e, seed as it comes from the gin.

This is the type of cotton most extensively raised and used in our country. Originally it was a perennial in the tropics but is now raised as an annual, growing to a possible height of 5 feet.

The fruit or "boll" contains a number of seeds, each covered with a long lint, when cotton ripens the bolls split open exposing the fiber. After picking, done by hand or machines, the cotton is ginned, to separate the fiber from the seeds. The lint is put into bales of about 500 lbs. each.

The seeds,—in this species covered with a short fuzz—are used for one of our most important food—oils, and for cattle feed and fertilizer.

245c Leaves with rounded tips. Fig. 271 ....
...................INDIA COTTON *Gossypium herbaceum* L.

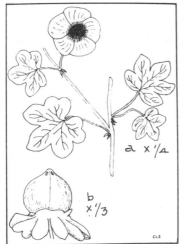

Figure 271

a, leaves and flower; b, fruit (boll).

This is the species of cotton most largely grown in China and Southern Asia. It is a smaller and weaker plant than either of the other two species described. The flowers are yellow with purple center; the seeds are large and angled. The lint is coarse and short and ranges in color from white to yellow and golden brown. Several other species of cotton are cultivated. PERUVIAN COTTON *Gossypium peruvianum* Cav. is grown in Peru and Brazil. TREE COTTON *Gossypium arboreum* L. is raised in Asia and Africa. It grows to a height of 10 feet with dark reddish-purple flowers.

246a Banana like plants, the leaves of which supply fibers........44b

246b Plants with long sword-like leaves arising in whorls from the ground or near it...247

247a Bearing a large fleshy multiple fruit as center. Fibers from leaves used for fine "pina-cloth." PINEAPPLE.....................44a

247b Leaves thick and fleshy; the source of fibers. Flowers and dry fruit on tall panicles. AGAVES...........................34a

248a Leaves simple 249

248b Leaves alternate, palmately compound, plants 3 to 12 feet high. Fig. 272............................HEMP *Cannabis sativa* L.

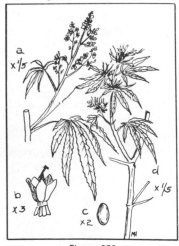

a, branch with staminate flowers; b, flower; c, seed; d, branch with pistillate flowers.

This rather attractive annual plant may grow to a height of 12 feet. It is of Asiatic origin but is widely raised for its tough stem fibers. It is known to have been used as a fiber plant for 3000 years or more.

The leaves are palmately compound and attain a length of some 9 inches. The greenish-yellow staminate flowers are borne in panicles often a foot high. The pistillate flowers are greenish and grow in leafy spikes on separate plants from the staminate flowers.

Figure 272

The plants are cut green and "retted" in water to free the fibers much the same as is practiced with flax for which it is substituted.

The fruit is a small globular achene which is used in poultry feed and mixed in canary bird seed.

The plant is often seen growing as an "escape."

249a Leaves about ½ as wide as long with serrate margins........250

249b Slender branching annual 1 to 4 feet high; leaves small, linear, entire. Fig. 273..................**FLAX** *Linum usitatissimum* **L.**

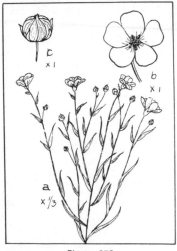

Figure 273

a, part of plant; b, flower; c, dry capsule containing the seeds.

This herbaceous annual growing to a height of 2-3 feet is a dual purpose plant, one variety being raised for its seed from which linseed oil is made, and the other for its fibers which are used for producing linen. The plants are cut very close to the ground (pulled in primitive culture) cleaned of its seed and dried. The straw is then "retted" by soaking in water for a few weeks or by spreading out on the ground to take the dew and rain. This is to loosen the f i b e r s which are removed, cleaned, bleached, spun and woven. The yield of flaxseed in our country in 1956 was 21,558,000 bushels.

The flowers are a beautiful azure blue.

NEW ZEALAND FLAX *Phormium tenax*, Forst. a member of the lily family furnishes fibers for cords and ropes. The leaves are often 9 feet long.

250a Herb or shrub 3 to 6 feet high, much branched. Flower small. Fig. 274........................**RAMIE** *Boehmeria nivea* **Gaud.**

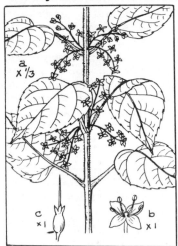

Figure 274

a, portion of plant with staminate flower; b, staminate flower; c, pistillate flower.

This herb or shrub, also known as Chinese Silk Plant, is much raised in China and India where it is native, and also in some warmer parts of Europe and America. Its height is about 6 feet. It has unisexual flowers, both types of which are borne on the same plant. The leaves have a white felt-like undersurface.

The fibers are removed from the stem and used to make a beautiful silk-like cloth as well as cord and paper. It is very strong, not readily affected by moisture and takes dye well. Chinese Grass Cloth is made from these fibers. Although a member of the nettle family, it does not have stinging hairs.

250b Annual to 15 feet high, branching only near top. Flowers, yellow, stamens many. Fig. 275......JUTE *Corchorus capsularis* L.

a, branch with flowers and fruit; b, flower; c, fruit.

This vigorous annual reaches a height of 15 feet. The leaves are characterized by ear-like basal teeth. The flowers are small and yellow. It is much raised in India and somewhat in other tropical countries.

The fibers are removed by retting as with flax and hemp. They are not as strong as either of these and deteriorate more rapidly. Jute cloth, twine and paper are its products. Burlap for bags, etc., is made from Jute.

NALTA JUTE *Corchorus olitorius* L. distinguished from its near relative by the elongate fruit has the same uses.

Figure 275

251a (b,c,d) Fleshy roots ground to fine powder for use as a dye. Leaves whorled in 4's to 6's, flowers greenish-yellow. Fig. 276. ....MADDER *Rubia tinctorum* L.

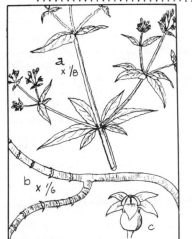

a, branch with leaves and flowers; b, piece of root; c, flower.

This plant which grows to a height of 4 feet has whorled leaves up to 4 inches long. The flowers are yellowish-green and rather inconspicuous. The fruit, a small fleshy berry is at first red and becomes black when ripe. The long fleshy roots are dried and ground to a very fine powder from which a highly permanent red dye is obtained. It has been largely replaced by synthetic dyes.

This plant found uses with the ancient Egyptians, one of which was coloring the wrappings of mummies.

Figure 276

251b Leaves used to make henna dye. Shrub to 20 feet; flowers very fragrant, white to red. Fig. 277.....HENNA *Lawsonia inermis* **L.**

a, branch with panicle of flowers; b, single flower; c, fruit capsule; d, seeds.

This shrub or tree growing to a height of 20 feet is valued as an ornamental as well as furnishing a dye for coloring nails and hair. Its small but very fragrant flowers are borne in conspicuous panicles. The flowers range in color from white to rose and cinnabar-red. The flowers are similar to the Crape-Myrtle one of the most attractive shrubs in our southern states. The leaves and flowers are used to make the Henna dye.

Figure 277

251c Nectar from large greenish-yellow flowers used for making perfume. Tree to 80 feet high; leaves 8 inches long. Fig. 278......
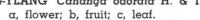
....................YLANG-YLANG *Cananga odorata* **H. & T.**

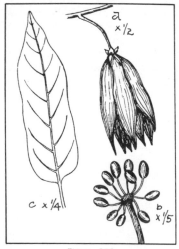

a, flower; b, fruit; c, leaf.

The very fragrant flowers of this tropical tree are the source of a famous perfume. It reaches a height of 80 feet. The greenish-yellow flowers are about 2 inches long and the many-seeded fruit is one inch long and colored green. It is a native of the Philippines, East Indies and Southern Asia but is grown in Florida.

The CLIMBING YLANG-YLANG *Artabotrys odoratissimus* R. Br. also known as "Tail-Grape" is a climbing tropical evergreen with flowers and fruit similar to *C. odorata*.

Figure 278

251d Trees with milky sap.....................................252

252b Sap used to make guttapercha. Fig. 279......................
..................GUTTAPERCHA TREE *Palaquium gutta* Burck.

This evergreen Malayan tree grows to a height of 40 feet. Its milky sap is collected by removing alternate strips of bark from the trunk and taking the sap as it exudes. It is prepared much as with rubber making, but lack the elasticity of that product. It makes a good insulater and water-proofer.

The leaves are about 4 inches long and covered with a dense rusty pubescence below, the flowers inconspicuous and the fruit a small fleshy berry.

× ⅓

Figure 279

253a Tall trees with simple leaves 5 to 12 in. long. Fig. 280.......
....................ASSAM RUBBER-TREE *Ficus elastica* Roxb.

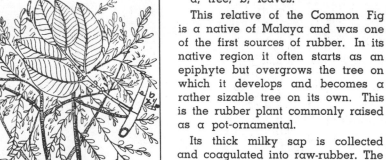

a, tree; b, leaves.

This relative of the Common Fig is a native of Malaya and was one of the first sources of rubber. In its native region it often starts as an epiphyte but overgrows the tree on which it develops and becomes a rather sizable tree on its own. This is the rubber plant commonly raised as a pot-ornamental.

Its thick milky sap is collected and coagulated into raw-rubber. The leaves are 5 to 12 inches long and leathery. The flowers are inconspicuous, with fruit yellowish-green and about ½ inch long.

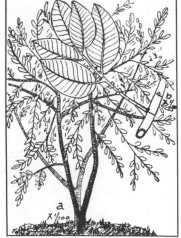

Figure 280

253b Tree to 60 ft. with compound leaves (3 leaflets) Fig. 281. . . . . . .
. . . .**PARA RUBBER-TREE** *Hevea brasiliensis* **Muell.**

a, tree; b, leaves and fruit.

This is our chief source of rubber. It is a native of the Amazon valley but is raised most extensively in Malaya and the East Indies. The tree attains a height of 60 feet, has leaves up to 2 feet long, white flowers and a woody fruit bearing 3 large seeds.

The milky juice or latex is secured by tapping the trees after they are six years old. Trees of this age and with much work of daily tapping and collecting produce about one pound of rubber per year.

Many plants have sap from which rubber could be made. A few that are so employed with some success are,—

Figure 281

MEXICAN RUBBER-TREE *Castilla elastica* a 60 foot tree with leaves 12-20 inches long.

CEARA RUBBER *Manihot glaziovii* a Brazilian 40 foot tree.

THE ECONOMIC PLANTS ARRANGED IN THEIR BOTANICAL ORDER

 AMILY trees or genealogical tables are often used to display the relationship of peoples. With similar purpose our economic plants are herein arranged in their logical order by families. This should give a better understanding of these plants and will serve as a convenient check-list.

How many of these plants could you recognize at sight? How many of them have you used for food? An interesting and profitable game for some social gathering might be devised from that.

DIVISION THALLOPHYTA

ALGAE

LICHENS

FUNGI

DIVISION PTERIDOPHYTA

DIVISION SPERMATOPHYTA

GYMNOSPERMS

ANGIOSPERMS

MONOCOTYLEDONS

GRASS FAMILY *Gramineae*

THE ECONOMIC PLANTS—BOTANICAL ORDER

HOW TO KNOW THE ECONOMIC PLANTS

THE ECONOMIC PLANTS—BOTANICAL ORDER

THE ECONOMIC PLANTS—BOTANICAL ORDER

HOW TO KNOW THE ECONOMIC PLANTS

INDEX AND PICTURED-GLOSSARY

A

Abaca 41
Acer 141
   nigrum 141
ACHENE: a dry, hard, one-seeded, indehiscent fruit. Fig. 282.

Figure 282

Adansonia 107
   digitata 107
AERIAL ROOT: roots arising from an above-ground part of a plant. Fig. 283.

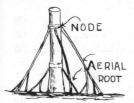

Figure 283

African Millett 26
Agar-agar 13
Agaricus 15
   campestris 15
Agave 34
Agaves 34
AGGREGATE FRUIT: a mass of carpels resulting from one flower, as in the blackberry. Fig. 284.

Figure 284

Air Potato 39
Algae 1
Algaroba 67
Allium 36-38
   ascalonicum 37
   cepa 38
   fistulosum 38
   porrum 36
   sativum 36
   schoenoprasum 37
Allspice 108, 134
Almond 59

AMENT: a tassel-like spike of imperfect flowers; catkin. Fig. 285.

Figure 285

American Black Currant 113
American Cranberry 114
American Elder 112
American Hazelnut 128
American Hop 137
American Plum 60
American Red Elder 112
Anacardium 133
   occidentale 133
Ananas 40
   comosus 40
Anethum 82
   graveolens 82
Angiosperm 17, 18
Anise 84
Annona 123, 124
   cherimola 123
   muricata 123
   reticulata 124
   squamosa 124
ANNUAL: a plant that matures and dies within one year.
ANTHER: part of stamen containing pollen. 9. Fig. 286.

Figure 286

Anthriscus 81
   cerefolium 81
Apium 79, 80
   graveolens 79, 80
   dulce 80
   rapaceum 79
Apple 65
Apple Mint 87
Apricot 58
Arachis 67
   hypogaea 67
ARCHEGONIUM: a flask-shaped, muticellular organ which bears the egg as in ferns. 1
Armoracia 43
   lapathifolia 43
Arrowroot 40
Artabotrys 152
   odoratissimus 152
Artichoke 101, 102
Artocarpus 121
   communis 121
Ascomycete 12
ASCOSPORE: one of several fungus spores borne in a sac-like structure. Fig. 287

Figure 287

ASCUS: a sac-like structure in which one to several fungus spores are borne. Fig. 287.
Asimina 123
   triloba 123
Asparagus 35
Asparagus 35
   officinalis 35
Asparagus Broccoli 45, 46
Asparagus Lettuce 99
Asparagus-bean 70
Assam Rubber-tree 153
Atriplex 146
   hortensis 146
Attoto Yam 39
Australian Bush-Cherry 109
Author 10
Authority 10
Avena 28, 29
   fatua 29
   sativa 28
Avocado 120
AXIL: the point on a stem just above the base of a leaf. Fig. 288.

Figure 288

B

Bailey 2
Banana 41
Banana Squash 96
Bunyan 122
Baobab 107
Barbarea 51
   verna 51
   vulgaris 51
Barley 29
Bayberry 108
Bean 69-73
Beech 132
Beet 139
Bell Peppers 91
Belleville Spinach 145
Benincasa 96
   hispida 96
Berry 6
Bertholletia 133
   excelsa 133
Beta 139, 146
   vulgaris 139
   cicla 146
Betula 140
   lenta 140
BIENNIAL: a plant that grows vegetatively one year and produces flowers, mature seed and dies the second year.
Big Shellbark Hickory 129

165

BLETTING: an over ripening
process. 63
BLUME: a whitish powder
sometimes covering fruit.
BOLL: seed capsule of cotton plant. 148 Fig. 289

Figure 289

BRACT: a modified leaf having one or more flowers
in its axil. Fig. 290

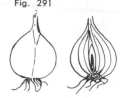

Figure 290

BULB: a bud with fleshy
scales for reproduction. 6
Fig. 291

Figure 291

BULBIL: (BULBLET): small
bulbs sometimes on fruit-
ing stems or in the axils
of leaves. Fig. 292

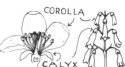

Figure 292

C

CALYX: the outer whorl of
floweral parts ;the sepals
taken collectively. 8 Fig.
293

Figure 293

CAPSULE: a dry dehiscent
fruit with two or more
carpels. Fig. 294

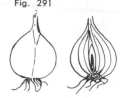

Figure 294

CARPEL: one section of a
pistil.
CARPELLATE FLOWER:
same as pistilate flower.
CELL: the individual struc-
tural unit of a plant. Fig.
295

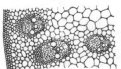

Figure 295

INDEX

Figure 296

Figure 297

Figure 298

Figure 299

Figure 300

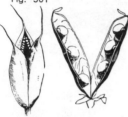

Figure 301

Figure 302

Figure 303

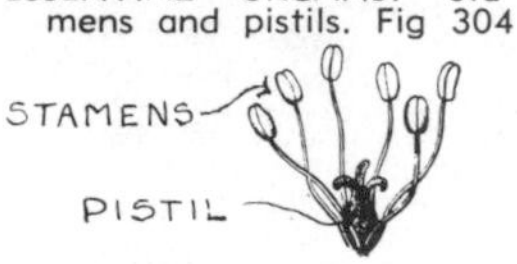

Figure 304

Figure 305

Figure 306

INDEX

Gossypium 147, 148
  arboreum 148
  barbadense 147
  herbaceum 148
  hirsutum 148
  peruvianum 148
Gourd 95
GRAIN: a one-seeded fruit with the thin fruit wall tightly adhering to the seed.
Graminea 18
Granadilla 104
Grape 116
Grapefruit 75
Grass Family 18
Green plants 2, 3
Ground Ivy 86
Ground Nut 67
Ground-cherry 92
Guava 107, 108
Gumbo 135
Guttapercha Tree 153
Gymnosperm 17

H

Hairy Huckleberry 115
Hamburg Parsley 80
HASTATE LEAF: with diverging lobes at the base of the blade. Fig. 307

Figure 307

Hawthorn 63
Hazelnut 128
HEAD: a dense cluster of sessile flowers arising from the end of a stem. Fig. 308

Figure 308

Head Lettuce 99
Helianthus 101
  annuus 101
  tuberosus 101
Hemp 149
Henna 152
Herb Patience 145
HERBACEOUS PLANT: not woody.

HESPERIDIUM: a hard-rined berry of the orange-type. 73
Hevea 154
  brasiliensis 154
Hickory 129
Hibiscus 135
  esculentus 135
High Cranberry 114
High-Bush Blueberry 115
Honey Bread 67
Hop 136
Hordeum 29
  vulgare 29
Horse Bean 69
Horse-Radish 43
Hubbard Squash 96
Huckleberry 115
HULL: loose outer covering of grain.
Humulus 136, 137
  americanus 137
  lupulus 136
Hungarian Millet 27
Husk Corn 20
Hyacinth-bean 70
HYBRID: the resulting cross of two species or strains.
Hyssop 85
Hyssopus 85
  officinalis 85
  alba 85
  ruber 85

I

Iceland Moss 14
Ilex 143
  paraguayensis 143
IMPERFECT FLOWER: having only stamens or pistil but never both. 10
INCOMPLETE FLOWER: lacking one or more of the following parts: sepals, petals, stamens, pistil. 10
INDEHISCENT: a fruit that does not open of its own accord. Fig. 309

Figure 309

India Cotton 148
Indian Corn 19
Indian Rice 28
Indian-fig 103
INFLORESCENCE: the natural arrangement of flowers on a stem.
INVOLUCRE: a ring of bracts under a flowering head. Fig. 310

Figure 310

Ipomoea 39, 137
  batatas 39, 137
Irish Moss 13
Italian Lovage 83

J

Jamaica Cucumber 98
Jamaica Pepper 108
Jambolan 109
Japan Plum 64
Japan Walnut 130
Japanese Apricot 58
Japanese Medlar 63, 64
Japanese Persimmon 105
Japanese Plum 60
Japanese Quince 64
Jerusalem Artichoke 101
Job's-Tears 23
Johnson-Grass 24
Juglans 130, 131
  cathayensis 130
  cinerea 131
  regia 130
  sieboldiana 130
Jujube 121
Jute 151

K

Kaffir 24
Kales 50
KEEL: the center pair of petals of a leguminous flower. Fig. 311

Figure 311

Kentucky Wonder 71
Keys 11
Kidney-bean 71
Kieffer 65
Knob Celery 79
Kohlrabi 43
Kumquat 73

L

Lablab 70
Labruscan Grape 116
Lactuca 99
  sativa 99
    angustana 99
    capita 99
    crispa 99
    longifolia 99
Lateral roots 5
Latex 8
Lawsonia 152
  inermis 152
Leaf Mustard 47

LEAFLET: one of the leaf-like parts of a compound leaf. Fig. 312

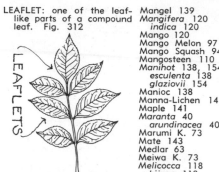

Figure 312

Leaf-stem 6
Leek 36
LEGUME: any member of the Pea family.
Lemon 74
Lens 68
   culinaris 68
Lentil 68
Lepidium 49
   sativum 49
Lettuce 99
Levisticum 83
   officinale 83
Lichen 14
LIGULATE F L O W E R: with strap-shaped or tongue-like corolla. Fig. 313

Figure 313

Lima Bean 72
Lime 75
Limequat 75
Linum 150
   usitatissimum 150
Litchi 119
Litchi 119
   chinensis 119
Liverworts 1
Locust Bean 67
Loganberry 55
Loquat 64
Lovage 83
Loveapple 91
Low Blueberry 115
Lucretia Dewberry 56
Lucuma 106
   nervosa 106
Lycopersicon 91
   esculentum 91

M

Mace 134
Madder 151
Maize 19
Mammea 119
   americana 119
Mammee-Apple 119
Mammoth Squash 96
Mamoncello 118
Mandarin Orange 77

Mangel 139
Mangifera 120
   indica 120
Mango 120
Mango Melon 97
Mango Squash 94
Mangosteen 110
Manihot 138, 154
   esculenta 138
   glaziovii 154
Manioc 138
Manna-Lichen 14
Maple 141
Maranta 40
   arundinacea 40
Marumi K. 73
Mate 143
Medlar 63
Meiwa K. 73
Melicocca 118
   bijuga 118
Melon 96
Mentha 87
   piperita 87
   rotundifolia 87
   spicata 87
Merliton 94
Mespilus 63
   germanica 63
Metroxylon 31
Mexican Avocado 120
Mexican Pinyon 18
Mexican Rubber-tree 154
Millet 25-27
Missouri Currant 113
Mitten Tree 139
Monkey Bread 107
MONOECIOUS: bearing only stamens or pistil in each flower, but with both kinds of these flowers on each plant.
Monocotyledon 18
Monstera 33
   delicosa 33
Morchella 15
   esculenta 15
Morel 15
Morelle 89
Morus 122
   alba 122
   nigra 122
   rubra 122
Mosses 1
Mother-of-thyme 86
Mountain Blackberry 57
Mountain Savory 85
Mulberry 122
MULTIPLE F R U I T: formed from several flowers. 6
Musa 41
   paradisica 41
      sapientum 41
   textilis 41
Muscadine Grape 117
Mushroom 15
Muskmelon 97
Mustard 46, 47
Mustard Family 42
MYCELIUM: the thread-like (vegetative) parts of fungus plants . 15 Fig. 314

Figure 314

Myristica 134
   fragrans 134
Myrtaceae 111

N

Nagami 73
Naked Oats 28
Nalta Jute 151
Nasturtium 142
Nasturtium 50
   officinale 50
Naval Orange 76
Nectarine 58
Nepeta 86
   cataria 86
New Zealand Flax 150
New-Zealand-Spinach 144
Nicotiana 89
   tabacum 89
NODE: the place on stems where leaves or flowers arise. Fig. 315

Figure 315

Nutmeg 134
Nutmeg Melon 97

O

Oats 28
Okra 125
Olea 135
   europaea 135
Olive 135
Onion 38
Opium 141
Opuntia 103
   ficus-indica 103
   tuna 103
Orach 146
Orange 76, 77
Oryza 27
   sativa 27
Ostrich-Fern 17
Oval Kumquat 73
OVARY: the enlarged part of the pistil. Fig. 316
OVULE: the part in an ovary which becomes a seed. Fig. 316

Figure 316

Oyster Mushroom 16
Oyster Plant 100

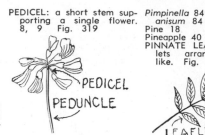

Q

R

RACEME: several flowers along the peduncle with each flower on a single pedicel. Fig. 323

Figure 323

RACHIS: the axis of a compound leaf or flower cluster. Fig. 324

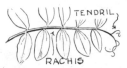

Figure 324

RECEPTACLE: thickened part of a flower stem to which flowers or flowering parts are attached. 8

Respiration 3
RETTING: using water to separate plant fibers. 8
RHIZOME: a fleshy, underground stem. 6 Fig. 325

Figure 325

ROSETTE: short stemmed plant with many radiating leaves. Fig. 326

Figure 326

S

SEPAL: one leaf-like part of the calyx. 8
SERRATE: saw-toothed margin of a leaf. Fig. 327

Figure 327

SESSILE: leaf or flower having no stem. Fig. 328

Figure 328

INDEX

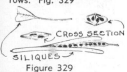

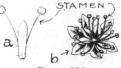

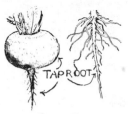